I Didn't Know You Were So Tall!

I Didn't Know You Were So Tall!

Insights and Stories from a Broadcasting Life

by Charlie Adams

Diamond Communications, Inc.
South Bend, Indiana

I Didn't Know You Were So Tall!

Insights and Stories
from a Broadcasting Life
Copyright © 2001 by Charlie Adams

10 9 8 7 6 5 4 3 2 1

Manufactured in the United States of America

Diamond Communications, Inc.
Post Office Box 88
South Bend, Indiana 46624-0088
Editorial: (219) 299-9278
Fax: (219) 299-9296
Orders Only: 1-800-480-3717
Website: www.diamondbooks.com

Library of Congress Cataloging-in-Publication Data

Adams, Charlie, 1962-
  I didn't know you were so tall! : insights and stories from a
broadcasting life / by Charlie Adams.
    p. cm.
  ISBN 1-888698-36-5
  1. Adams, Charlie, 1962-   . 2. Sportscasters--United
States--Biography.   I. Title.
  GV742.42.A33 A29 2001
  070.4'49796'092--dc21

                                    2001037175

Table of Contents

Dedication

This book is dedicated to the memory of sportscaster Paul Hartlage...my broadcasting mentor and my friend.

WHAT'S IN A NAME?

The title of this book has to do with the comment I get at least 1,000 times a year as a local TV News anchor.

"I didn't know you were so tall!"

I'll be walking in the grocery store to buy rock salt, which is as good as it gets in life, and three or four people who recognize me from the local TV newscast will say those exact words to me.

"I didn't know you were so tall."

I'll shrug and wait for the next comment, which always comes.

"You don't look that tall on the News."

I explain how that since I am 6' 6" the other anchors sit on large city telephone books, or they simply levitate.

We chuckle, and I move on to buy rock salt.

I can deal with the "I didn't know you were so tall" comment. I'm an adult now. What was tough was growing up with the name "Charlie."

Much to my surprise, the name "Charlie" is popular with new parents these days. My son Jack has lots of friends named Charlie. It's sort of cool.

When I was growing up, I think I was the only young Charlie on the mainland. I guess there was Charlie Sheen, but that was about it. Everybody named their kid Scott, Karen, John, Mary, Lisa and other normal names. I got Charlie, which really wasn't so bad until that blasted, but effective, tuna commercial came out with the "Sorry, Charlie" line. I was scarred for life!

I was in grade school when everybody started seeing that commercial. My fate was immediately sealed. Anytime I missed a shot in basketball practice I heard, "Sorry, Charlie, only the best tasting tuna makes baskets."

"Sorry, Charlie" this. "Sorry, Charlie" that. I wanted to go get a shotgun and fill that Tuna's butt, or at least his fins, full of buckshot.

That wasn't the only hurdle I faced with being named Charlie. The "Peanuts" cartoon strip was big time famous. Of course, the main character was Charlie Brown. He was a good guy, but he wasn't exactly James Bond or Warren Beatty when it came to "suaveness." Having the same name as him linked me to such things as having a football lifted up just as it was about to be kicked. People often asked me "how Snoopy was" and other amazingly original and witty things like that.

I guess, looking back, I had the opportunity to escape "Charlie" by going with my official first name of "Charles." Ugh. What ten-year-old wants to be called Charles?! When I picture a young boy named Charles, I think of somebody that plays the piano all day, has slick stuff in his hair, and enjoys eating vegetables as a kid.

Personally, I think all very young Charlies should come up to the older Charlies and say, "Hey, you endured the tough times of Charlie Tuna and Charlie Brown... you made it possible for us to be Charlies without dealing with all the joking about our names. You blazed a trail."

The "Sorry, Charlie" thing will never end. Recently, I was in an edit booth at WSBT-TV in South Bend, Indiana when always-focused news reporter Denise Bohn whipped open the door to edit. She quickly realized I was in there and backed out to find an open booth.

"Sorry, Charlie," she said as she left. I winced. Painful childhood memories came flooding back! I almost fell to the floor in a fetal position and whimpered. At least she didn't bring up that blasted sassy tuna.

Going by Charlie was tough enough in the "heyday" of Charlie Tuna and Charlie Brown. Can you imaging what life would have been like for me had my friends learned my middle name was Floyd?

That would have been the end of me. I would have had to join the circus and feed the elephants. Thankfully, I kept "Floyd" a deep, dark secret. If that had slipped out, I would have endured the "Floyd the Barber" comparisons from the "Andy Griffith Show." And, of course, "Pretty Boy" Floyd of mobster fame.

Speaking of names, I am awful at remembering names. At least I am an equal opportunity name forgetter. I forget everybody's name at first. I am so caught up in meeting the actual person that the name slips me.

Personally, I think we should all have our names stamped on our foreheads. It would make small talk so much easier during the holiday party times. Nametags just tarnish the heck out of a spiffy suit or beautiful dress, so I say we have our names tattooed on our foreheads.

One thing that has saddened me about names is how some names are being forgotten because, in all honesty, they are sort of gooberish. I'm talking about names like Buster, Otis, Bertha and Earline. You just don't see yuppie parents in the suburbs naming their boy "Berferd" or their girl "Irma" anymore.

As my way of preserving those names, I have used my position as local TV News guy to honor them. From time to time, I will use a story for our 5:30 News off the National Video Feed. The feature story will have people in it from different parts of the country. Viewers in our neck of the woods don't know them from Adam. If I can't find their names on the computer, I create some names for them. Heck, I create names for them even if I can find their names on our computer. I always use names like Bud, Hugo, Pearline, Luther, Gus, Elrod, Otto, Leeoddis Oatmeal, Percy, Earl, Lester, Helga, Jim Ed, Herbert, Ethel, Herman, Mortimer, Merle, Mo, Chester, Bubba, Ernestine, Cletus, Vern, Marcel, Barney, Claude, Tito, Beauregard, Bo-Ceefus, Onus, Cooter, Toots and so forth and so on. It's my hope that maybe an expecting mother watching the news will pat her tummy and say, "I am going to name you Berferd, sweetie."

People in the public eye have their names changed often for professional reasons. Someone named Rudy Poot in real life would want that changed legally if they were going to be the main News Anchor of a TV station. I once knew a boy named Lee Peed. No kidding. I don't know what kind of work he went into, or if he changed his name. His whole family should whack that last name—change it to Evans or something.

Years ago, a fine young broadcaster named Lance Ghos worked for me as a weekend sports anchor. The news director at the TV station worried that viewers would call him "Casper the Ghost" (as if grown people out there would sit in their living room saying, "Honey, Casper the Ghost is on doing Sports!"). Lance had to come up with a new on-air last name, so he picked up the 1988 *Big Ten Football* magazine and skimmed through it. Michigan State's quarterback was Bobby McAlister, so Lance picked McAlister and has used it ever since. He is now a successful sports radio host in Cincinnati.

When Lance worked with me in South Bend, we did a weekly Thursday night sports talk show, which was sponsored by Burger King. One night we were set up at the downtown South Bend Burger King when some "weathered-looking" fella in a dark green, dirty trenchcoat walked in and sat down at our table. Much to our surprise, he proceeded to slip on the headsets reserved for guests and calmly start telling our radio listeners that, "The Russians were coming."

I didn't know if he meant they were coming to get Whoppers or conquer our nation, but I had to remove the headsets and send him on his way. We calmly got back to talking Notre Dame Football and at no point during the show did Russians ever show up in downtown South Bend.

If they had, maybe they could have given me tips on remembering names.

COFFEE AND COIFFURES

For the most part, I'm a pretty content guy. I'm not picky about food in a restaurant. My steak always "looks fine." It took me about an hour to determine my last car. I really didn't care what color it was, as long as it wasn't teal. But when it comes to coffee, I'm an odd duck. Now, I know a lot of coffee drinkers "have to have coffee when we get up." I'm like that too. That's pretty universal. I've got to have my coffee at a certain hot temperature.

No exceptions.

For example, each weekday I walk to the South Bend Chocolate Café downtown. It's right next to the College Football Hall of Fame. They have lots of great coffee flavors, but as soon as they see me coming, they know what to do. Someone says, "What's the most recently brewed? Here comes Charlie." Someone from the back room comes out and feels the jugs, and determines the hottest coffee. Even if it's Tropical Raspberry Toffee Coffee, that's what I drink. It's got to be steaming. I recently strolled in, and the lady behind the counter looked at me and said, "Colombian and Vanilla Nut." Those were the two freshly brewed coffees. We both laughed. I said, "Vanilla Nut."

Another oddity is that I must pay for my coffee and get my change before it's poured. Some of its "hotness" could be wasted sitting there as the cash register work is done. I drink my coffee in the Cafe. Do I use the nice mugs they offer customers? No. I ask for the Styrofoam "to go" cups because they maintain heat better than the tastefully done mugs. I am the only one who drinks coffee in the Cafe in a "to go" cup.

5

When I am in a 7-11 mini-mart type store, the clerks probably think I'm loopy. I go back to their coffee area, grab a medium Styrofoam cup, and take it back up to the cash register. I plop it down and say, "I'm going to get a medium cup of coffee." They always wonder why I don't have coffee in it at that time. They ring me up. I put my change in my pocket, and I go back and pour my coffee. To make sure it's hot I always put it in the microwave and zap it for about one minute. I get all bent out of shape when I can't find a microwave in those stores. I'm like Dustin Hoffman's character in *Rain Man*, who went wacky when he couldn't watch his favorite TV show every day at the same time.

One time, in a mini-mart, I could not figure out the microwave. My coffee kept going round and round on that silly clear turning plate inside. I don't know the scientific explanation, but the coffee blew up and splattered all over the bottom of the microwave. Being a good citizen, I cleaned it up.

Microwaving coffee in the mini-marts always irritates the construction guy waiting next to me to nuke his burrito. I just shrug, get my coffee scalding hot, find a lid to contain the heat, and hustle to my car so I can start driving before the coffee goes through significant heat reduction.

When I am at friend's houses, I get coffee and then march straight to their microwave. It has to be hot. I read where actor Al Pacino feels the same way. Maybe his coffee is what gets him so wound up as an actor.

One time my two children and I were going to watch someone's house for the night. I couldn't take the risk that they didn't have a coffeepot, so I loaded my own in the car and took it over. Gotta have that coffee right away or else I start doing the shimmy shake and quake and get all squiggeldy.

In restaurants, when the waitress comes by for a refill, I say, "Whoa." I ask that they either pour out my original cup, or I slide over an unused cup. There will be no pouring onto used coffee, because it has lost much of its hotness. The old coffee blunts the new.

At the TV station where I work, I don't drink coffee. I stick to bottled water. Between coffee and bottled water, basically my life is one trip after another to the men's room. Our veteran anchorman Luke Choate is in charge of what he calls "The Water Club." Apparently, he lines up the delivery of the water, and handles payment of it. Personally, I think the station pays for the water, and Luke has a little scam going to pad his pockets. Ha! He can't fool me. It finances his new golf clubs. Every time I turn around, Luke is hitting me up for four bucks. I'll tell him, "Luke, I thought I just paid my monthly dues!" He'll smoothly say, "Oh, you were late on last month's payment. This month's is already due." Nancy Sulok of the *South Bend Tribune* does regular columns in which she often investigates things. I think she ought to check out Cool Hand Luke and his Water Club.

Luke was WSBT's 5:00, 6:00 and 10:00 News Anchor for many years. Because he was so popular with viewers, the station put him in charge of the Community Relations Department. He still anchors the noon newscast, but has a different schedule these days. I went digging around for it and would like to share it with you now.

Luke's Schedule:

Get up. Breakfast on his deck overlooking the river. Head to Erskine Golf Course for nine holes. Pop into WSBT. Check messages. If there are any community requests, pass them on to Charlie, "since he does those 'Making a Difference' stories." Stand in hall to make sure general manager Bill Sullivan sees him. When seen, head to the Driving Range at Bobick's. Then back to WSBT by 11:30. Glance over noon newscast scripts.

Anchor noon news. Then, lunch at The Summit Club downtown. Back to work. Tell secretary Patti Hostetler that he is closing office door to make community calls. Once in office, work on putting or take short nap. Around 3:00, stand in hall to be seen by Bill Sullivan again. Around four, slip out to get in nine holes at Blackthorn. Next day: Repeat schedule but with different courses and LaSalle Grill for lunch.

My man Luke has good poofy-woofy TV News hair. Me? I've got half-thick hair and some thinning hair. Growing up, I never thought I'd lose hair. It was so thick as a kid that people called me "Brillo Head." Then, in 1990, at age 28, I was in East Lansing to cover Notre Dame at Michigan State. I was sitting in our satellite truck, which has multiple mirrors. For the first time, I happened to see my hair thinning on the crown of my head. I was stunned. I think I missed kickoff because I kept running my fingers through it and angling my head around the mirrors to get a closer look. Viewers that knew me kept walking by the truck and wondered what I was doing.

For several years, it didn't recede much. Then, it started thinning on top. Can't have that. I'm on TV News! Got to have Ken Doll hair. So, I started the battle against it. Rogaine came out and I got some. I think it was doing a pretty good job, but advertisements of other stuff got my attention too. Basically, they were snake oil, but I tried them. One "serum" would pour down my forehead and leave bright red streaks making me look like a warrior Indian. I couldn't leave the house until they disappeared. As the years went by, Propecia came out. Just a pill. Seemed simple to me. I tried it for awhile, but just couldn't believe that pill knew just where to go to grow hair. I was worried it would miss the mark and hair would start growing on my forehead. It had already dealt with red streaks, and could not handle anything else.

Rogaine works for a lot of men, I believe. Maybe not everyone. I saw where NBA star Karl Malone of the Utah Jazz was doing commercials for Rogaine. Then about a year later I saw where he had shaved his head bald. Maybe he wasn't patient. I have found that applying Rogaine like you're supposed to can be a challenge to my daily schedule. The instruction pamphlet says not to wash your hair for four hours after putting on Rogaine in the morning. Okay, let's say you get up at 7:00. You apply Rogaine at 7:01. That means you don't get in the shower until 11.

"Hey, boss, this is Charlie. Yeah, you know how I've been coming into work at 9:30...well, Rogaine is in my life now and I need to start coming in just before lunch."

I think bald people could turn their hair loss spot into a revenue producer. Companies could come up with little round product signs that would cover bald spots. They would have tiny suction cups that would cling to the head and stay put in winds up to 20 miles per hour. Mazola Corn Oil could sponsor the bald round sign for example. Mazola would pay the person $500 a year to wear it only at times when they are around a lot of people.

Examples: Amusement Park visits, trips to New York City, sports events and concerts. If the person were just going down to the deli to get a sandwich, there would be no obligation to the sponsor to wear it.

As I lost some hair, I became sensitive to comments like, "That other man has lots of great hair." Now, what exactly did he do to have a lot of hair? It's a genetic thing. Someone told me it goes back to your mother's father. My mother's mother was married five times, so I don't believe I ever saw what my hair-decider-man looked like, but the bottom line is we don't earn great hair. Now, I could see it if, when we were kids, we would end up with great hair as adults if we avoided sweets, ate asparagus twice a day, and helped five little old women across the street twice a week. But that's not the way it works. You're hair blessed or you're not. What really gets my goat are guys like my friend Mark Bradford, soccer writer for the *South Bend Tribune*. He has more hair than he will ever need. You can't see his scalp because it's so thick. By law, he should have to give me some because I am in broadcasting.

I use shampoo that says **Big Thick** Hair Shampoo on it. That's always fun to take on trips where others see it. If I was not on TV News, I think I'd buzz my hair. It's wavy, has a widow's peak hairline, and a cowlick. It's one adventure after another every day. There was no reason for God to come up with cowlicks.

Here is how I think God should work hair loss for men. Have the baldness start at a very early age, say four years old. Then, as the man ages, he gains more hair. That way, he has something to look forward to as he gets older. The way it works now, a man loses his hair slowly and dreads his hair-status five, ten years down the road. Under my plan, a man could look forward to having thick hair in, say, his late 40s. Granted, a first-grader would look a little odd with extreme male pattern baldness, but the hair payoff would come later in life. A youngster could simply wear a football helmet or shower cap for years until the hair came in.

"AND THE WINNER OF THE NOBEL PEACE PRIZE IN LITERATURE..."

With the release of my first book in 1998, *Travels with Charlie* (NOT the Steinbeck book! That's "Charley") came my first book signing. For big-shot authors, signings are old hat, but for me, this was my first and I was nervous and wound up. To make sure people would actually be there, I wrote folks at church and said, "Be there, please."

It was a beautiful winter Saturday in mid December in South Bend. Snow was falling. People were celebrating Christmas. My first signing was at Media Play in Mishawaka. It was set for 1:00. I had to mail some Christmas presents, so I left my house around noon and went by the Post Office. A big line was waiting me there, so I got a little behind on my schedule. I headed towards Media Play around 12:45. I knew basically where it was, but as I got close, I took a wrong road and had to find a way to get back on the right track. As I was looking across towards Media Play I ran right into the back of another car. "BONK!" It was a minor fender bender, but one that still required us both to stop and get out and go, "Hmmm. Mmmm. Look at that. Hmmm." The fella was a nice enough guy. He was not filled with road rage. Still, he wanted to call the police. When he said that, I gulped. My book signing was about ten minutes away!

"I understand you want to call the police," I said, "but I have a book signing in ten minutes." He looked at me like, "Yeah, right buddy, and I've got a date with Sandra Bullock in fifteen minutes."

"No kidding," I pleaded. "I really do. It's just over there at Media Play. Can we take care of our business over there?"

He went "Hmmmph" and "Mmmmphf" for a bit and reluctantly agreed. "I'm still going to call the police over there," he assured me.

"Oh, wonderful," I thought. "My first signing and the police will show up to talk to me." Beggars can't be choosers. I was just glad we were leaving the scene of the bump and getting away from all those glances that people give you when they drive by.

We got to Media Play and there was a decent-sized line. Okay, many of those in line were from my church. Friends from Elkhart were in it, and my boss Meg Sauer and her husband John. But there was a legitimate line. My heart was still out of whack from the stress of the fender bender, but I sat down and started signing away. The guy I bumped stood off to the side with one eyebrow raised. I did not ask him if he wanted to purchase a book. After awhile, he came over and said, "I won't worry about calling the police. Here's my insurance card. We'll deal with it on Monday." How 'bout that? He was a nice guy, after all.

Over the course of my promotions for *Travels with Charlie* I had many memorable experiences. Most of them were humbling. One of the exciting things about writing a book is seeing it go on various web sites, like Amazon.com. I was thrilled to see the book on their site. Then, I looked at the details. It said my book was number 375,439 in sales on Amazon.

Oh, my. I didn't know there were 375,000 books out there. I would call friends and say, "Order a book off the Amazon site. One sale and my book will probably go up to number 350,000 in sales!"

Book signings could be eye-opening, too. At a signing at Northridge High School in Middlebury, I was sitting at a table in the lobby signing books. Well, at the time, I was just sitting there. No one was buying. The school had put a poster up of me and the details of the signing on the thick beam next to me. During half time of the basketball game, a student didn't realize I was sitting there. He stared at the poster of me and turned to his friends and said, "*He* wrote a book?"

Yes, many times I got reactions from people along the lines

of, "If Charlie can write a book, anyone can." I found the experience of selling books at a signing to be a little like selling a used car. After the initial long line was finished, I was usually looking at an hour of folks drifting in and flipping through the pages. I would sit there and yap about the book in depth. They would go "Mmmm" and "Hmmmm" for ten minutes. Then, they would put it back down in front of me, smile, go inside the store and buy some other book.

Of all the signings I did, I think the nicest people were those at churches. I gave a talk at First United Methodist church in Mishawaka, then wandered over near my trusty box of books and sat down to sell a few. I think the whole group got up and formed a line. I quickly sold everything that was in my box and had to ask a fella there to take my truck keys out to the parking lot and get more books. They went through those books in no time flat. I don't think it was my book that was the big draw. They were just kindhearted people who wanted to support what I was doing. Had I brought plastic armadillo's in there I'll bet they would have formed just as long a line. Maybe longer.

My most uncomfortable time was when I did a signing with two professional authors.

Between them, they had written and illustrated many books. I was on book number one. I felt like an impostor sitting between them at Waldenbooks. I kept thinking the Book Police would show up and slap cuffs on me. "Let's go, big guy. What do you think you're doing sitting here with these pros? Let's go downtown."

I took my two children to many signings so that they could be exposed to books and reading. Many times they would be in the back of the bookstore being read to by a store assistant while I was out front selling books at the furious pace of, oh, about three per hour. Then one day four-year-old Abby sat down next me at the table just outside of the door. Cute as a button, she promptly drew a crowd and my book sales shot up. When she asked me if she could go back to the back of the store and be read to some more, I said, "No!"

"Why not, Daddy? Didn't you want me to be read to by the nice lady?"

"Uh, Daddy needs you out here. Now, uh, let's prop you up where people can see you better as they go by."

Once you write a book, you quickly learn that four out of every other five people either want to write a book or have written a book. They just need some help getting a publisher.

Of course, when you write a book, you want to promote it and give it the best exposure possible. I had no qualms about going into a bookstore and taking my little book from the Indiana/Regional section and mischievously gliding over to *The New York Times Best Seller* shelf and putting it over whatever was the number one book. That's right. Tom Brokaw's *Generations* book got covered by my paperback a time or two. I never did cover up those "I Was in the Mob" books for fear of getting whacked.

Eventually, my book was moved from the prime exposure of the front part of bookstores and was placed in the Regional section, which is where books go after the initial buying surge is over. From time to time I would pop in to encourage the ones still on the shelves. I found myself wondering if they would ever go through "Price Reduced." They didn't for two years, then at one bookstore it happened. I walked in one day and "50% OFF" was stuck on the covers. Agh! The self-esteem of those books was so low. They felt worthless. They started carousing with Joan Collins' books late at night. Morally, their lives went south. I encouraged them and told them it wasn't just them! Many of the regional books that were two years old were 50% also.

"Just look at the Sammy Sosa book next to you," I said to my books.

A lady down the aisle looked at me funny.

My books looked at the other reduced books, and felt better. Except for one book.

"Maybe if you hadn't changed tense so much in us, we would have been reviewed better and sold more," that one book told me. He was a smart aleck book. I picked him up and put him next to the old Monica Lewinsky book.

"No! Don't put me there," he squealed as I plopped him down. "I'll never sell here!!"

13

ADVENTURES IN BAKERSFIELD

My first job as a TV News sports anchor was in Meridian, Mississippi, home of actress Sela Ward. For those of you who don't know who Sela Ward is, shame on you. Her recent phone company commercials are reason enough to enjoy life.

Anyway, I hadn't been in Meridian long when Wayne Kilmer, the general manager of KBAK-TV in Bakersfield, California called to offer me a job. No interview. No reason to fly out there. He had seen my tape. Liked it. Wanted me out there. Wayne appeared to be a man who got right to the point. As a young man of 22, I looked at the map, saw it north of Los Angeles, and said, "Sounds good to me."

Driving through Barstow, California, I started to have my doubts. No city should be named Barstow. I entered Bakersfield through the seedy side, which is not the best way to form a good impression. KBAK-TV was a very nice, modern station, though. Upon arriving, I discovered I would have my own office down the hall from the Newsroom. The reason for that was the sports director before me, Bob Fields, got on the nerves of everyone in the newsroom so much that they moved him out and down the hall. Bob was actually a very creative and energetic sports anchor, who would go on in his career to become a news director in Milwaukee.

I didn't get to stay in my private office long. A new news director came in and decided he wanted the office. He didn't want to be in the actual newsroom, where it would seem a news director should be. He wanted my digs down the hall.

One day I came to work and all my stuff had been moved into the engineering room! There was a little side room in there that this guy determined would be the new sports office. Needless to say, we didn't get along too well. I found him to be quite annoying. He did get his just reward for evicting me in such fashion. Once a week, he and the co-anchor Jerri Fiala would have animals on the news set. Usually dogs and cats, but one time they brought a snake in there. This guy was letting the snake slither around his shoulders when it pooped all over his suit. I'll bet you never thought about how a snake poops. Well, this snake went to town all over his clothes. Without getting too graphic, I will say it was white and contrasted poorly with his navy clothes. He had to shed his suit jacket for the rest of the news. I almost burst a gut laughing so hard. Viewers that tuned into the hour newscast mid-way and missed the snake pooping started calling our newsroom to complain that, "Your news anchor is not wearing a suit jacket."

Since Bakersfield was just an hour and a half from Los Angeles, I made frequent trips to cover the pro teams there (this was back when they actually had NFL in LA). The first time I covered a Lakers game, I sat down in the media room to get a bite to eat. While pouring over the Lakers press release, Jack Nicholson sat down right next to me to eat some soup. As I recollect, he didn't speak. He just ate his soup, with minimal slurping. Jack would spend time in the media room for privacy before going to his courtside seat.

I loved to do video camerawork, so with my photog credential I was able to shoot the Lakers game from right under the basket. Laker cheerleaders to my left. Laker cheerleaders to my right. Good enough reasons right there to enter broadcasting. Actress Darryl Hannah was ten feet away from me. She was very nice and carried on a conversation with my buddy Steve Schill, who I had brought down with me from Bakersfield. He was our weatherman. After the game, we headed to the Lakers lockeroom where Steve did the camerawork and I did the interviews. Steve didn't really know camera work. Hey, he was a weatherman. I started the camera, put it on his shoulder, and told him to point it at the face of the interview subject. We weren't exactly *CBS Sports* on location. I was impressed by how nice and accommodating the Lakers were to us. I asked Magic Johnson to grab our KBAK microphone, look into the camera, and recite some lines that would have him be judge of our "Friday Night High School Basketball" show back in Bakersfield. He was more than happy to do it, and had fun with it. James Worthy and Byron Scott could not have been nicer to us. Even Kareem, who was known to be aloof, said "Sure," when I asked him to do an interview. While we made the rounds in the lockeroom, actor Rob Lowe came in. This was in 1986. That was in the days of the Brat Pack. The players all shook his hand. From what I was told, all Hollywood actors wish they were pro athletes, and all pro athletes wish they were Hollywood actors.

During my three years in Bakersfield, I also made trips down to cover the Clippers. Agh, you say! The Clippers?! Well, not so much to cover the Clippers, but their opponents. During Dr. J's last season, I got KBAK engineer Pete Capra to go down with me to cover the Clippers-Sixers game. KBAK was a small station. There weren't enough news photogs to take on weekend LA trips, so I would get buddies like Pete and weatherman Steve to go with me. A quick lesson in Camerawork 101 and we were cooking!

Pete got some odd looks in the Sixers lockeroom after the game because his hair went halfway down his back and he wore earrings. He also had a floppy white T-shirt on. Our sole reason to be there was to do a story on Julius Erving. The high-flying Doc was just weeks away from retirement. We waited patiently off to the side as Sixer players showered and started leaving the lockeroom. Dr. J was answering questions from the print media. I leaned in and asked him if I could do an interview. I told him we had come down from Bakersfield and wanted to do a special story on him. He said to please hold on, and he would do an interview with me after he showered.

Dr. J did everything with grace, and that included taking a shower. It took him awhile. He must have made sure every pore was cleansed. We waited, and waited. The entire lockeroom cleared out. Sixer players were on the bus waiting to ride to the airport. I turned to Pete and said, "Pete, it doesn't look good for our interview. We're just Bakersfield. He'll probably say he doesn't have time." Pete said, "Dude, that would be a bummer."

Sure enough, as Dr. J left the shower, some equipment guy told us we might as well leave because as soon as Doc got dressed, the bus was leaving. Dr. J heard him as he walked our way and spoke to all of us as he got to his locker.

"These young men have come a long way to interview me," he said, while looking at the equipment guy. "I am going to answer their questions as soon as I get dressed."

I looked at the equipment guy like "go eat a Philly Cheese Steak." He shrugged and left. We waited as Dr. J meticulously dressed. When done, he gracefully answered all my questions about his career. He then shook our hands firmly and gracefully walked towards the bus.

The bus left when Doc was ready.

In 1987, weatherman Steve and I went down to cover the Bulls at the Clippers. The sole reason to go was to interview some young player named Jordan. I did the camera work from right under a basket. Charles Oakley plowed into me on a fast break. Jordan soared all over the place. The LA Sports Arena had more people cheering for the Bulls than Clippers. Afterwards, I approached Jordan to do an interview. I was nervous. He sensed it. He said, "Hey, sit down and I'll answer whatever you want." I'm sure they were questions he had heard a hundred times before, but he respectfully answered them, and it turned out to be a fine story.

I also got down to LA to cover the Rams and Raiders on a regular basis. Rams running back Eric Dickerson, now on the *Monday Night Football* announcing team, would see us in the lockeroom and say, "The Bakersfield boys!" One time, while doing Rams interviews, a fellow broadcast journalist came up to me with a problem. He was the ESPN West Coast reporter. His photographers' batteries had surprisingly run out of energy. They couldn't do any more interviews. He asked if they could borrow one of our batteries. I said, "No problem." The reporter was Jim Gray. Perhaps you know him as the man who would go on to join NBC and conduct the famous Pete Rose interview. Whatever your impression of him now, he was tenacious and hard working back then. Gray broke the story of Dickerson being traded from the Rams to Indianapolis. That was his big break that helped him get to network.

I also took buddies from work with me to cover the Dodgers and Angels. Vince Stokes, a Chicago native, was one of our production workers at KBAK. A sports nut, he went with me to cover the Angels one time. Reggie Jackson was with the team. Of course, I had to try to interview Reggie, so I approached him during batting practice. He hardly acknowledged me. I don't think "I'm Charlie Adams of KBAK-TV Bakersfield" impressed him too much. So I thought about it for a moment, and went back to Vince, who was near the batting cage with the camera. I said, "Vince, he spurned me. Here's my idea. I'll run camera. You go up and ask him to do the interview. He will see that you are a young, black broadcaster and want to give you a break." Vince agreed, and walked over to Reggie. He asked him to do an interview. Reggie hardly acknowledged him, too. Vince walked back over. "So much for your theory of a brother wanting to help another brother," said Vince.

Moving on, I went over to phenom rookie Wally Joyner and asked him to come over and do an interview when he had a chance. He mumbled something. It didn't sound promising. Ten minutes later, I was standing there with Vince, when Joyner started walking to us from the batting cage and Reggie started walking to us from first base.

"Oh, great," I told Vince. "They're both coming at the same time." I didn't know what to do. Reggie and Wally looked at each other as they got to us. Reggie promptly turned around and headed back. I never did interview him, but Wally turned out to be a fine interview.

I truly enjoyed my three years of sportscasting in Bakersfield. Former Indy car racer Rick Mears and "Hee Haw" star Buck Owens are both from there, as are Frank Gifford, formerly of *Monday Night Football*, former Packers lineman Ken Ruettgers, and former Denver Bronco Louis Wright.

A ton of folks from Oklahoma have moved out there over the years because of the oil. There are so many Sooners out there that our station carried "The Barry Switzer Oklahoma Football Show." It got great ratings. I'm talking about a California station carrying the OU football show!!

One time famous drag racer "Big Daddy" Garlitts raced near Bakersfield. On the Monday following the race, he made an appearance at a local auto parts store. His dragster was on display in front of the store. It was long and low to the ground. However, behind the driver's pod, a wing-deal went pretty high. I went out to interview Big Daddy, who really was a small pappy. The photographer got us to walk around the dragster for video that would go into the story. Well, I was so caught up in what Big Daddy was saying as we walked behind the dragster, my head smacked right into that rear wing. I looked like José Canseco trying to play outfield. I fell back and just about fell on the asphalt. Big Daddy probably thought, "typical sports guy."

Gary Miller was the sports director of the NBC affiliate KGET-TV in Bakersfield. An exceptional writer, Gary also had the good looks and sports knowledge. I knew he would be headed to a larger market. Gary and I got along great for competitors. Heck, we used to call each other before the 11:00 News and exchange scores we had been corralling from area high school basketball games. Sure enough, Gary was hired by KCNC-TV in Denver. He quickly became established in that sports-mad city and has gone on to do exceptional coverage of the Broncos. In fact, when speculation was swirling that John Elway was going to retire, Gary was in San Jose covering the Colorado Avalanche against the Sharks. Gary learned that Elway was in that area playing golf. He found out where, got his photographer, and tracked down Elway on the course. Gary got the exclusive interview of Elway talking for the first time about retiring. In 1998, Gary became the first local TV News sports reporter to become a full-time NFL specialist. That's how big Broncos coverage is to his station and his market. I've always felt South Bend and Green Bay should have full-time, nothing-but-Irish/Packers reporters.

One day, I was in the KBAK sports office when someone from the Rio Bravo Country Club Pro Shop called me. "Charlie," he said. "I have a tip for you. Actor Burt Lancaster is out here right now playing a round. He came up from LA. Don't tell anyone I told you, but you may want to come out." I rounded up a photographer, and out we went! We tracked Lancaster down on the fifth hole. He was playing in blue jeans, which seemed like something an actor would do. They have their own drum beat, you know. I respectfully approached him (after he made a good shot and was in a good mood) and asked for a short interview. He obliged, and gave a wonderful description of the fulfillment of being an actor. After that one answer, I thanked him and let him get back to his "escape from LA" round of golf.

One Friday morning, photographer Mike Derryberry and I headed out to the big lake near Bakersfield. The national drag boat races were going to happen that weekend. I'm talking about those speedboats that flat-out *fly* across the water. Dangerous as can be! We were done interviewing some of the racers and Mike was taping the boats speeding across the lake.

Suddenly, one lost control right in front of us and flew into the air. It flipped completely at a high speed and crashed back down into the water. People started screaming. Emergency boats sped out to the wreck. I knew it was bad. Really bad.

The driver had been killed instantly. We waited at the dock area as they brought in the torn-up boat. I was suddenly in the midst of a big, breaking news story. We started interviewing fellow drivers. I was surprised how cooperative they were. I figured they would issue a lot of "No comments." The racers I talked to were very open about how death is a real possibility in their sport. They knew how fast they went. They accepted the consequences. They stood grim-faced on the bank knowing full well that it could happen to them one day.

I ended up being the lead story on every newscast. The coverage ended up winning the Golden Microphone Best Spot News Award for our division in southern California. Obviously, it's an award I wished we had never won because of what happened to the racer.

I was able to go down to Los Angeles three times for the Golden Microphone awards. I won the Class C Best Sportscaster award a couple of times. Seeing as how our competition was Santa Barbara and some other market, that's not exactly bragging. Each time I went down, I spent time talking with a certain KTLA-TV sportscaster named Keith Olberman. He did the most riveting four-minute sportscast I had ever seen, or probably ever will see. This was before he did *ESPN SportsCenter* with Dan Patrick. Olberman would go on to be outstanding in the one-hour format of *SportsCenter*, but you should have seen him when all his talents and writing skills went into a four-minute sportscast. I would stop producing my sports at 10:45 at night to watch him come on the LA station. I didn't try to copy him. I think everyone should be themselves on TV. But I certainly enjoyed watching him.

Since our sports staff was small at KBAK, I was always recruiting people to help us out. I often got a man named Bill Funk to go down to Los Angeles with our sports reporter when our local school, Cal State Bakersfield, was playing an LA school. Our sports guy would shoot the game. At half time, he would give Bill Funk the tape and Bill Funk would drive to KABK-TV where they would uplink the tape to me in Bakersfield. Bill Funk was a man of limited financial means. He drove an old van that looked like a pirate ship. He also had a crusty gray beard and a glass eye, so he looked like a pirate. He sort of looked like Quint in *Jaws*. Remember the guy who slid down into the shark's mouth near the end? Often times, Bill Funk would show up at KABK with the tape and they wouldn't let him in because they were scared off him. He was not the ideal representative of KABK, but he was a good man and a true friend. He would do anything to help us out. I spent many days floating down the Kern River on an innertube with Bill Funk and other buddies.

Bakersfield was home to the Class A Bakersfield Dodgers. They played at Sam Lynn Ball Park. From the outside, it looked like a fort in the Cowboys/Indians days. We had a lot of stories to cover at ol' Sam Lynn. One day the Bakersfield Dodgers general manager called and told us Sandy Koufax was there to give advice to the pitching prospects. Sandy did not do newspaper interviews at that time. Someone must have written a disagreeable story, but he was good to us. We got an enlightening interview with him back behind the stadium where he could keep his privacy.

My weekend sportscaster was Greg Kerr. Sharp as a tack, Greg was, and is, as good a writer and hard worker as I have seen in broadcasting. One summer weekday, Greg was shooting highlights of the Bakersfield Dodgers for the 11:00 News.

Somewhere along the line Greg had told me he had wanted to be a baseball umpire. He had gone to the Harry Wendlestedt Umpiring School and had graduated. Well, as Greg was getting ready to tape the game with one of our cameras, the home plate umpire got woozy. The field umpire came in, and it was determined that the home plate guy couldn't go. He was sick as a dog. Several conferences ensued and they didn't know what to do. They had to have two umpires.

Greg put his camera down and went over and told them his background. Both managers listened, and everyone agreed to let Greg—the local weekend sportscaster—be the field umpire. They went to the Umpires room and got Greg some clothes that sort of fit. He looked a little rumpled. I picked up the camera and taped away as Greg made the calls on the basepaths. He did all right. One time his call got the opposing manager all bent out of shape, but he dealt with it fine. I ended up doing a story on the 11:00 News that night on Greg's sudden umpiring experience!

Probably the dumbest thing I did in Bakersfield was...well, actually there were two things. First, my friend Dan Tudor and I went up to San Francisco for a few days to see the Giants, Alcatraz, and all those kind of things. One night we decided to go to a comedy club. Earlier in the day I had bought a San Francisco shirt and was wearing it. The comedian spotted me and started grilling me. I did look like Joe Tourist. Then, I made an awful mistake. I liked Bakersfield, but it was the butt of many jokes in California. Just the name—Bakersfield—is enough material for several jokes. Anyway, this cat asked me where I was from. If I had any sense, I would have said "Santa Barbara" or something. But no, I said Bakersfield. My buddy Dan Tudor elbowed me like, "You asked for it." Sure enough, that sent the comedian on a five-minute, Rodney Dangerfield-like barrage on me.

The other boneheaded thing I did was make a prediction on the news one night. Bakersfield and Garces, the alma mater of former Packer Ken Ruettgers, were high school football powers. Garces was a smaller school, so one night I predicted Bakersfield would beat them in the upcoming big game. Of course, I was there on the sidelines covering it. It was a rainy, muddy night. Garces ended up beating BHS. Afterwards, I was doing interviews on the field when suddenly a bunch of guys tackled me. Scared the heck out of me. At least ten of them grabbed me and started hauling me to the sidelines.

"You're going to pay for picking us to lose," said one of them. It was then that I spotted the massive mud puddle by the twenty-yard line. I knew I was about to get very dirty. Being the savvy, marketing-minded TV guy, I said, "Whoa! Do what you must, but I must summon my photog over here to get this on tape!" They showed mercy enough to allow him to come over. Then, they started rocking me back and forth. One! Two! Three! Weeeee! Up I went into the air, and down I went into the mud. Splat! My on-air clothes were a mess. Everybody howled. I just got up and wiped the mud from my eyes. It was in my ears. My hair. Yuck.

Like most Friday nights, we were on deadline, so we raced back to the TV station, and I trotted out there and did all the Sports in my mud-baked clothes. I looked like I had just come back from The Homeless Convention, but I was a sport about it, and learned not to pick against Garces!

It was in Bakersfield that I fine-tuned my prankster abilities. In fact, I just about caused a co-worker to croak because of one of my antics. We had a very intense news reporter named John Patton. Highly respected by me and everyone else who new him, he took his work extremely seriously. He jumped on a news story lake an Alabama tick on a lazy dog.

One day I heard John and a photog were covering a story near a sports event. I asked them to pop into the sports event and get a little video of it on the way to their news story. They agreed and got some video of the story. They then went on to what became a very big news story. John got back to the newsroom in his normal focused state. I always got a kick out of how intense he got on big stories, so I decided to have some fun with him. I approached him as he zoomed around the newsroom getting ready to write his big story. I asked for the tape so that I could take it back to sports and dub off the sports material they had shot earlier in the day.

John looked at me like I had asked if I could drive his car off a cliff.

"You do know that there is serious news video on this tape?" he asked me while staring through my head.

"I know, John, I will be very careful with the tape. I'll dub off the sports stuff to another tape and get this tape right back to you."

He wasn't crazy about the idea, but reluctantly agreed.

I hustled back to the sports office and got another tape that looked just like the one with the vital news footage on it. I then pulled out the tape and fixed it to where it dangled from the tape shell with rips in it.

Taking a deep breath, and etching concerned wrinkles on my forehead, I went back to the edge of the newsroom and prepared to "get" John. I slowly walked into the newsroom and stood in the middle. John was at his desk typing his story as deadline loomed. He looked up as I stood there with a ruined tape.

He turned as white as a polar bear. His jaw dropped. He really thought it was his actual news tape.

"John...I started to edit, and the tape just scrunched up. It tore. I...feel awful about this."

He slowly rose up.

"The good news, John, is that I was able to dub off the sports stuff. Well, I'm going to go get a snack in the break room. See ya."

I thought he was going to kill me. The vein on his neck turned aqua teal. Those tiny blood vessels on his nose threatened to burst. He moved towards me with intent to, oh, cut my head off, when I pulled the real undamaged tape out of my pocket.

Everyone laughed.

John just stopped in his tracks and kept looking wide-eyed at the tape, me and everyone else.

Flailing his arms, he scooted back to his desk, probably thinking he was destined to keel over from an anxiety attack if I kept pulling pranks on him!

I left Bakersfield in 1988 to go to WSBT-TV in South Bend. Ironically, I was able to return to southern California shortly to cover #2 Notre Dame at #1 Southern Cal. In November of 1988, the two arch rivals played a big game that was pivotal in Notre Dame's march to the National Championship (maybe their last ever, the way ND Football has been going lately...). WSBT sent photographer Mike Pease with me to Los Angeles. Mike grew up in Bluffton, Indiana. He went to Southern Wells High School. Mike had never been to California. I'm not so sure he had ever been out of Indiana. After covering the game on Saturday, we had some time off on Sunday before flying back to South Bend. We drove out along the shores of Malibu. Mike said he was hungry, so we pulled into one of those California eateries that has sushi and people concerned about ozone. We walked in and the hip, tan, lean Californian host sized us up with an odd look on his face. Mike was wearing white short pants and black church socks. His legs were whiter than white. The Californian asked Mike where he was from. Mike grinned and said, "I'm Mike Pease and I'm from Bluffton, Indiana!!"

The guy looked at Mike and said, "I didn't think you were from out here."

KEEPER OF THE NEWS ROOM

A conversation with Assignment Desk Operator John Snyder of WSBT-TV

CHARLIE ADAMS: I'm here with WSBT-Television Assignment Desk Operator John Snyder. John, explain to the readers what all you do in your job.

JOHN SNYDER: It's interesting that you use the title "Assignment Desk Operator." That's what I feel like sometimes...a switchboard operator. We get hundreds of phone calls a day in here. Sometimes I'll have calls stacked up and waiting like the jet approach to O'Hare. We could use a full-time receptionist.

This really is the catchall job. You're responsible for the big stuff, like pairing up and assigning reporters and photographers to cover stories, and to keep track of the coverage throughout the day, and to enter future stories into the file that we keep on each day. You run the editorial meetings for the staff. You do reporter schedules. You spend tons of time reading each piece of mail that comes in, each fax (and we get them by the forklift-load), news magazines, you scour the newspapers, look at other news organizations on-line, watch the wire services, schedule the satellite and microwave crew trips, and plan out future events.

But, you also have to cover the little human quirks that, left uncovered, will make your operation grind to a halt. Little stuff like making sure certain people get their lunch breaks because you know they get surly without it. Running an earpiece out to a forgetful reporter, offering to move some news cars that have the satellite truck blocked in, pull road maps and get driving directions for crews so they don't get lost. I try to remember who got beat up the most on overtime or emotional stories or in bad weather last week so that the misery is spread around to someone else this week. And maybe most importantly, listening. I'm not talking just about the police scanners or to the breaking story hidden inside a "crackpot" call. It's tough being in the field. I did it for 13 years. It rains on you, it snows on you, it sunburns you, bugs bite you, cops give you tickets and people yell at you—a lot. Nobody likes the media, unless you're doing something to, in some way, help them make money or feed their ego. It requires a tremendous amount of physical and mental stamina to be in the field five days a week. When someone who is under siege needs a place to vent or a shoulder to cry on, a lot of times, it falls to "The Desk." Someone should do it. It's tough out there.

You have to keep coming up with new ways to say, "I know your life stinks right now, and there's not much I can do to change it—the show still has to go on—but I do think you're an incredible, strong fighter, and just hang in there, I respect you."

It's a very adversarial position sometimes, being sort of the buffer zone between upper management and the rank-and-file, so it is especially rewarding when you can do something to make someone's day go better. For example, making sure they get off early to make a date or a family function or a flight for a vacation or a car show. It's also really fun to give a crew a story they really want to do, like a NASCAR race for a NASCAR nut, or a piece on a steam train or a World War II plane for a history buff, or a celebrity interview to someone who is a fan.

CHARLIE: As you mentioned, John, you get a lot of phone calls from viewers during the day. Share with the readers some of the most bizarre and gut-wrenching calls.

JOHN: You get your garden-variety paranoids and hostiles like anywhere else. The ones that haunt you are the true hard-luck stories that you just can't do much about—like old ladies who can't pay their electric bill or people who are sour about custody battles. The custody calls have renewed my commitment to do anything I can to not put my kids through that.

The calls that really drive me nuts are the callers who "...heard something from a friend of a friend about a health segment...something about a new treatment...not even sure it was your station that aired it...a couple of months ago." You have no idea how long it takes to track that kind of vague request down...and I assure you, time is one thing we don't have to spare. It also bugs me sometimes that people really continue to assume the worst about us. I can't speak for the networks or other markets, but WSBT-TV really does make a concerted effort to do positive stories on people making a difference, good athletes, good students, good schools. We make major, major commitments to Friday night high school sports coverage. We do Town Hall Meetings, e-mail feedback on the air, "Sketch the Sky" weather contests for school kids, "I Love to Read" promotions, the Science Fair, segments on community arts festivals, the "Women's Show," "Connecting with Kids" and "Making a Difference" on the 5:30 News, and just a host of other positive community things. Still, I take calls from people who say we do nothing but bad news, think we're conspiring to undermine American values, that we're all biased, that we're all idiots, really inflammatory stuff. I know how hard we work to be balanced. Some days, insults like that don't roll off your back as easily as others. I've learned to remind myself the remarks are made in anger and not aimed at me. I do agree, though, with the callers who think "Mr. Food" may someday track them down and kill them.

CHARLIE: What advice would you give people who are thinking about going into TV News?

JOHN: Seriously, I think you need to give solemn thought to what you're committing to before you ever go on your first interview. Call, get to know, e-mail people whom you admire and who are in the business now. Work to get the real story about what they think. Tell them you're serious about making the call one way or another for a career track. I teach some courses part time in Radio and TV Production and Announcing, etc. I tell all the kids in the first class to get something straight. That is, yes, there are stars who make a bunch of money, and if you're blessed with the face of Matt Lauer or Deborah Norville, you can skyrocket to the top, bypassing a lot of other folks clawing their way up. For the rest of us, though, and even to the Matts and Deborahs to some extent, it is a messy, grueling crawl that will take a whole-life commitment, if you're serious about doing well in the business. I like to tell the students that it's a lot like going into the priesthood. A precious few people work so-called "business hours," and when you're new in the business, you should count on working every Christmas, every Thanksgiving, every New Year's, every Memorial Day, every Fourth of July, every Labor Day, most weekends, a lot of overnights. The pay will be awful at first. I know of some people who were starting out who reported in the day and waited tables at night to make ends meet. For every Peter Jennings and Katie Couric you see on the air, there are hundreds of drones slogging out an existence behind the scenes. I don't say that to be negative, but I see so many interns come through the WSBT-TV newsroom with the glow of certain stardom in their eyes. No one ever gave them the real story, and they crash really hard into reality.

I still think the cream rises to the top, though. People who will do well in this business also pay their dues, but their talent is recognized early on, and they rise quickly. If you do stick it out, it can be especially rewarding. There is no other job I know of that will give you such a well-rounded view of the world. You brush elbows with all walks of life, the criminal underbelly, the heads of state, the political operatives, the cops, the homeless, the teachers, the athletes, the zealots, the motivators, the parasites, the bureaucrats, the business leaders. You see our government, our legal system, our schools, and our culture in both all their glory and all their warts. Stereotypes fall fast. You start learning that everything that was so black-and-white in college is a lot more shades of gray now in life. I guarantee you that if you're an earnest, hard-working street reporter you will at least come out a better human being on the other side. Again, that's if you're earnest about being a journalist, and not just a TV star.

CHARLIE: John, elsewhere in this book I am accusing WSBT-TV noon anchor Luke Choate of running a Water Club scam. It seems he is *always* asking for dues in the Newsroom.

JOHN: What's he up to, Charlie?! I'm not making any accusations here, but let me just say that the timing of the beginning of the Water Club and the purchase of Luke's riverside condo have always been curiously close. Don't tell him I said this, but I think he comes back at night and just fills those water jugs from the fountain upstairs. He probably has a roll of "sealed" stickers hidden in his desk.

CHARLIE: Thanks for taking the time to do this Question and Answer session. John, please leave the readers with some parting thoughts.

JOHN: Oatmeal isn't really "instant." It still takes hot water. Integrity is important. It is important in you as a viewer. If you don't like what you see on TV, it is, in a real sense, your fault. TV only programs what people watch. As soon as the ratings say the junk you hate isn't popular with viewers, it will disappear...quickly. But, for all the talk, we Americans are hypocrites. We hated the O.J. coverage, but stations that dumped the wall-to-wall daily coverage lost in the ratings. Carol Marin trumpeted a return to basic, true journalism on WBBM-TV in Chicago, after her falling out with WMAQ over the Jerry Springer debacle. Her more integrous newscast has been rewarded with ratings lower than ever. That just reinforces to the owners and consultants that they were right about tabloid TV in the first place.

More than that, though, some funerals in the last two years taught me something else about integrity—maybe it would be better to say "priorities": It's not really so much the people from the office who show up at your funeral. It's the people in your family; it's your bowling buddies, your school friends, the people in your church, the guy at the hardware store, the owner of your favorite restaurant. As much impact as the media has on this culture, it will still be your day-to-day contact that really makes the difference—one person at a time. Being a friend, being faithful with a smile, shoveling the neighbor's walk, teaching a Sunday School Class, are the real acts of chivalry. After January, Bill Clinton will fade from everyone's memory. Fifty years from now, it will be hard to remember who was President today. Your kids won't forget who was daddy or mommy by then. And besides, Bill Clinton would never come over to help you paint your house.

To spend more time with his wife and three children, John recently left TV News for a flexible sales position. John also teaches a broadcast communications course at Bethel College in Mishawaka, Indiana.

INDIANA WEATHER

It is a Sunday night in December in South Bend, Indiana. The weather is calm and clear. The temperature is 33 degrees. Weekend meteoroligist Bob Werner stands in the WSBT-TV Doppler 22 forecast center.

The veteran pores over data as weekend news anchor Jim Pinkerton strides into the office. "I don't like to be an alarmist," Werner says to Pinkerton while glancing down at the StormTracker equipment, "but we've got quite a situation developing here." Pinkerton looks at the graphics and maps generated by the high tech equipment, worth hundreds of thousands of dollars. Various colors fill the screens representing the magnitude of something significant headed for northern Indiana.

"The computer models are developing this," Werner says as he points to the weather pattern on the screen, "and they all point to a big bulls-eye on our chest." A panhandle hook has developed over the panhandle of Texas. Loaded with moisture from the Gulf of Mexico and with cold air behind it, the area of low pressure is hooking towards the northeast and is headed straight for the WSBT-TV viewing area. El Niño weather patterns kept this kind of hook away for the past couple of winters, but nothing was going to stop this one.

"A winter storm is brewing in the southwest tonight and it is barrelling its way towards Michiana," Pinkerton says to viewers at the top of the 11:00 News. He quickly gives way to Werner, who addresses viewers from inside the weather office.

"There is a winter storm warning for Monday, Monday night, and Tuesday," Werner says quickly and clearly. "We could have as much as 17 inches of snow by early Tuesday. An icy mix is possible. Winds up to 15 to 25 miles per hour and temperatues in the 20s could make this a dangerous situation tomorrow, to say the least."

At 3:30 in the morning, Meteoroligist Jennifer Schram arrives at the forecast center to carry the torch from Werner, who has stayed late to keep an eye on the developing storm. Schram immediately gets to work preparing the forecast for the morning TV news. As someone who cares deeply about the WSBT viewers, Schram focuses on trying to warn the viewers without causing any kind of panic. For two solid hours, she periodically checks radar and satellites while she analyzes the upper level and surface charts. She looks at soundings, which provide information from weather balloons sent into the atmosphere and compares computer models. Specifically, she tries to pinpoint the track of the Low so that she can determine who will get the most snow.

At 5:30, the morning newscast begins. Morning anchor Tom Halden quickly tosses to Schram in the forecast center.

"Stay at home if you can," Schram advises viewers. "Doppler 22's StormTracker is already showing freezing rain in Springfield, Illinois, and snow in Chicago. The messy weather is headed our way. By mid morning, the snow and some sleet will really be coming down. We expect between 14 and 20 inches by this time tomorrow. The National Weather Service is issuing a blizzard warning for tonight. To make it worse, lake effect snow could mix with this tomorrow. Please stay with us throughout the day and we will keep you informed on the winter storm warnings."

At 8:15, News 22 Executive Producer Tim Ceravolo brings the producers of the noon and evening newscasts into the morning conference room. The good natured kidding that normally accompanies the beginning of these daily meetings is absent. A businesslike expression is on everyone's face as Ceravolo speaks.

"This is going to be one of those defining days," he tells them. "We have to provide information for the viewers."

Assignment Editor John Snyder, who has helped guide coverage of many winter storms, quickly lists the reporters and photographers working that day. Story ideas are exchanged. Ceravolo jots down every idea.

"I think we should have one crew live at the Meijer store on Bremen Highway," Snyder says. "It is near the bypass. They could get reaction from people going to the store, and show the travel on the bypass."

Ceravolo nods approvingly.

"We could put Denise or Dawn on people stocking up at stores," says 5:30 PM Producer Jennifer Addington.

The ideas keep coming. Ceravolo fills up a sheet of paper.

"We could have a Supreme Court ruling about the Presidential deadlock also," says 5:00 PM producer Jerry Siefring.

"At least we don't have a shortage of strong lead stories," Snyder says as the meeting breaks up and everyone moves to the heart of the newsroom. There, reporters and photographers wait to learn their assignments. Ceravolo quickly moves to the large planning board and leads discussion on assignment specifics. More ideas are shared. Ceravolo then starts laying out the coverage plan.

Reporter Dawn Clapperton and photographer Ryan Flory will cover road conditions. They will do a live shot on the noon news at the Meijer near the bypass. Reporter Erin McElroy and photographer Zach Mark will cover people stocking up in case a blizzard does hit. Reporter Denise Bohn and photographer John Rabold will cover the heavy snows expected in southwestern Michigan. Reporter Ray Roth will cover the LaPorte County and Marshall County areas. Ed Ernstes will cover Elkhart.

Ceravolo writes all of this down on the planning board. Each team is told what is expected of them for the various newscasts. He then writes "Supreme Court issue" down and the other stories of the day.

"Charlie Adams is doing a story on Logan Center for our '22 Ways of Giving' series," Ceravolo says. "That will air at 5:30 along with his story on the pressures gifted teens feel." That story is part of the "Connecting with Kids" series that airs every Monday, Wednesday and Friday.

The meeting ends at 9:15 and crews immediately head to the field. Ceravolo then informs the engineers and production workers that he wants Schram to do live weather reports during CBS programming all morning. They will be every half hour. Schram will keep them to one minute if she can.

Morning anchor Tom Halden leans back from his desk and speaks to everyone. "I just got off the phone with John Schalliol, the airport director," Halden says. "He says other than two incoming flights from Detroit and Cincinnati, all of the airlines are in the process of shutting down operations for the day. Visibility is down to zero."

In the newsroom, the phone rings off the hook. Linda Leszczewski handles the bulk of the calls, which are schools and businesses calling with cancellations.

"A woman just called to remind people to take care of their dogs that are tied up outside," Leszczewski says out loud. She then enters all the cancellations into the high-tech system the station has for such severe weather days as this. Instantly, cancellations go to the lower part of the television screen.

Long before this storm, Leszczewski had mailed every school or business to inform them about the station's exclusive automated system where they could simply call with their specific cancellation information. They were given a number to dial, then an access code and ID number to enter. Many businesses and schools call the number and don't worry about calling the newsroom to talk with someone specifically. By 9:30 AM, 16 closings have been entered. Everything from bingo at Holy Family School to the closing of school systems.

News Director Meg Sauer informs the newsroom that at 11:00 *CBS News* will break into WSBT programming for a special report on the US Supreme Court hearing. She lets the editors know that on Telstar 6-1E (digital KU) they can get audio tapes from the hearing, and on Telstar 6-3B they can get video of sketches of the hearing. There is a feeling nothing major will come out of the hearing on this day, which is a relief with the magnitude of the local weather.

Sauer then lets all departments know that the live weather cut-ins will continue all afternoon. They will continue to be at the top and bottom of the hour and promo commercials will be dropped from programming for more weather cut-ins if needed.

As the phones continue to rattle, Assignment Editor Snyder gets off the phone. "Mikki Dobski says that Mayor Luecke is declaring a snow route clearance condition. He may declare a winter weather emergency condition later today."

Upstairs, WSBT General Manager Bill Sullivan sends out an e-mail to all station employees: "This is a very busy time for the news room. They are being inundated with telephone calls. Supervisors, if you or any of your employees can help out, please let Meg or Tim know. Also, with conditions as they are developing, supervisors can allow employees to leave early this afternoon."

Shortly afterwards, help arrives. Pat Fogarty of sales quickly learns how to help enter closings information in the computers.

Meanwhile, out in the field, reporters and photographers battle the snow and dipping temperatures as they shoot their stories. The snow has arrived and is coming down steadily. Photographer Ryan Flory has had times in the past where his camera has frozen in the field. One time the mast of the live truck he was operating froze at its highest point. It had to be lowered for them to leave. Ryan used a blow dryer to warm up the mast and then climbed up on it and hung and swayed it back and forth until is came loose.

On this day, Ryan will work 15 straight hours. He will shoot stories and do live shots for the noon, 5:00, 5:30, 6:00 and 11:00 newscasts. He knows it is part of the business. Photographer Isaiah Cooks once had the eye piece of his camera freeze around his eye when he was out in bitter cold weather. The camera wouldn't come off his face. He had to awkwardly get into his news vehicle and turn on the heater full blast. What few people were nearby walked by awkwardly as they looked in at a man leaning down with a camera stuck on his head.

"One time I was out getting video in real cold weather," Cooks recalls, "and these three dogs came running by me. I didn't pay much attention to them, but when I got back to the news vehicle, they had jumped inside to stay warm. I didn't know if they were wild, so I called the police to get them out."

At noon, co-anchor Debra Daniel looks into the camera as the red light comes on signalling the start of the newscast. "It is ugly out there; a winter storm is blasting Michiana today. The roads are packed with snow and very slick. Good afternoon. I'm Debra Daniel."

"And I'm Luke Choate," says her co-anchor, who tosses to Schram in the forecast center.

"A winter storm warning is in effect," Jennifer says. "Wind chills tonight will be well below zero with visibilities down to a quarter mile. The wind will be gusting to around 30 MPH and that's why there's a blizzard warning tonight. By tomorrow morning, some of you will see 14 to 20 inches of snow on the ground."

After Jennifer's forecast, the anchors toss live to reporters at various sites. Much of the half hour is focused on the panhandle hook and its wallop. Back in the forecast center, numerous e-mails come in about the storm.

Who in thunder sent all of us to Siberia or worse?! We had sleet and gobs of it here at Chapman Lake north of Warsaw. Our poor pup knows it's really slippery outside and "will hold it" until he thinks conditions improve! Maybe Spring!! The weather is not even lousy here today. It's PUTRID! — Peg Scott, viewer

Could Rick, Jennifer and Bob explain the different colors seen on radar during snow storms as they do when we have rain? — Ed Switalski, viewer

Great weather coverage! We're down here in Culver and we have so much ice you can't stand on your own two feet. Please send some snow our way. We would much rather have two feet of snow instead of this ice! — Tammie, Tonnia and crew, viewers

As the afternoon goes on, the snow gets worse. By midafternoon over 200 cancellation calls have been taken. Assignment Editor Snyder works with various reporters to get the information crucial to viewers. At 4:17 Snyder sends out this information to reporters: Folks, here is the latest with respect to snow emergencies or snow warnings. Be careful to distinguish the differences between cities when you do your live reports. Not every city has banned parking, travel, etc.

South Bend has declared a snow emergency as of 6 PM. The mayor has enacted the snow route parking restrictions.

The mayor and police department are asking citizens to not drive unless it is an emergency, but Capt. Williams says they are not ticketing drivers who are on the road.

Mishawaka's mayor is asking everyone to stay home unless it is an emergency, but no snow emergency has been declared. The city has activated its third ambulance to handle extra emergency calls.

Elkhart's mayor is asking residents to stay off the streets and not park in the streets. He says 20 snow plows are out now.

Tragically, the bitter cold conditions lead to the death of a local man. 71-year-old Gerald Pawling collapses after shoveling snow at his home and can't be revived after having an apparent heart attack. This story will lead to the newsroom later doing a story on precautionary measures to help prevent such a terrible thing from happening again.

In the forecast center, chief meteorologist Rick Mecklenburg utilizes his Doppler StormTracker equipment and does periodic cut-ins all afternoon. Days like this are fascinating for Mecklenburg, as he confesses that he stayed up all night in anticipation of the big storm. One minute viewers will be watching "Dr. Laura" on TV, and then the next minute Mecklenburg pops up on their screen with the latest information.

"StormTracker has been flawless," he tells a producer in the office. "See the yellow picture here on the screen? That's heavy snow. The green is moderate. We can tell people how it's moving. It's going to snow like crazy all night. This is not like lake effect snow. Everybody is getting this one. It will be close to a blizzard. A blizzard warning has been issued for four counties because the wind is going to be so high. It all depends on the angle the wind blows. You can have a blizzard with just four inches of snow because of the wind."

Mecklenburg has brought in extra clothes. He anticipates staying long after the 11:00 News and will probably sleep at the station. Like a captain of a ship, he wants to be there during weather like this. His evening dinner is packed and ready to eat in the office. He won't leave the building at all until the next morning when Schram comes in.

In the newsroom, News anchor Cindy Ward works the phone relentlessly pursuing information. She learns when major businesses are closed, and works with others to find out when the area's major malls close. Shortly before 5:00 she goes to wardrobe and joins Debra Daniel to anchor the 5:00 News, which will have an extra-large viewership because of the weather.

"Good evening. I'm Cindy Ward."

"I'm Debra Daniel. We have live reports from all over Michiana tonight. And on the bottom of your screen the latest school and business closings."

For the next 90 minutes, the teamwork clicks to near perfection as Mecklenburg clearly explains to viewers what has happened, and what will happen. Reporters describe conditions out in the field. The station's sky cameras are activated to show viewers what the Toll Road and other locations look like from the sky.

At 6:30, when the newscast ends, those involved in coverage merely catch their breath. The storm is getting worse as darkness settles in. News Director Meg Sauer lets all departments know they will keep doing cut-ins twice an hour throughout the evening. She announces that extra crews will be coming in for the morning news coverage and that they may preempt the *CBS Morning News* with Bryant Gumbel to focus on the weather, if that is warranted. Sauer stays late to help coordinate coverage with Snyder and Ceravolo and the producers. Pizza is ordered because everyone involved in the coverage won't have time to go anywhere to eat.

By 7:30, over 400 closings have been sent in or called in to WSBT. To get on air, they have to affect at least 50 people. "Poker at Vern's house" does not warrant getting on the bottom part of the TV screen. There are so many legimate closings that the scroll at the bottom of the screen takes a long time to get to every closing. Sauer calls Tom Labuzienski in sales to get the okay to run the scroll over commercials as well as programming from 7:30 to 8:30, which helps that situation.

South Bend turns into a ghost town as northwest winds of 29 miles per hour lead to a wind chill of 12 below zero. Reporters and photographers are given new assignments for coverage for the 11:00 News. Reporter Dawn Clapperton rides with snow plow driver Rodger McFall as he helps clear the city roads. A bolt of lightning startles him as he answers questions while driving.

The State of Indiana sends 20 snow trucks to South Bend from down state to help the local trucks. Clapperton learns this and makes a note to say that to viewers as a tag to her story on the 11:00 News.

Though many of the stories have to do with the elements outside, the news desk assigns reporter Kirk Mason to follow the story of how new South Bend schools Superintendent Dr. Joan Raymond is handling school closings. Some parents were rankled earlier in the day when Raymond would not close school until the end of the school day. Mason goes on to report that Raymond fears some small children let out early won't have proper care at their home. Mason also reports that in the past, South Bend schools have waited until the morning to announce closings for that day. Raymond, he says, is different in that she makes the decision the night before when she has enough information in front of her.

By 11:00 twelve inches of snow have dumped on South Bend and more has fallen on southwestern Michigan communities. At 11, Mecklenburg shows viewers how the cold air coming across Lake Michigan is going to lead to lake effect snow into the night. "We're getting a one-two punch," Mecklenburg says as he draws on the screen to represent what's happening. He tells co-workers later that nights like this are a lot of fun for weather "geeks" like himself.

Co-anchors Cindy Ward and Debra Daniel throw to reporters at different locations. The reporters then introduce their respective reports, taped earlier in the evening. The coverage is flawless. When later viewed, it is rated as award-winning caliber news coverage.

When the 11:00 News ends, Mecklenburg stays on to monitor the weather. He continues to do cut-ins until Schram arrives in the wee hours. With Schram settled in, Mecklenburg heads home at 2:00 AM. His car promptly gets stuck in the snow and it takes him three hours to get out! The snowstorm continues to pummel the area deep into the night. News

Director Sauer, after staying late to help guide the evening coverage, comes back to the station at 6 AM to help with the crucial morning news coverage. Viewership shoots up on mornings like this as viewers watch to see closings and the latest forecast.

Cassopolis, Michigan residents wake up to 16 inches of snow. To the south, Plymouth deals with just eight inches. Viewers continue to call the newsroom with information and even story ideas. One caller tells of a family who lives next to a local business. He says they have no alley access, so in the winter they park at a local bank. He says despite the No Parking signs the family has okayed it with the bank, but that a Grinch-like plow driver blocks their car in with snow.

The caller says, "The driver does it just to be mean."

That's his theory, anyway.

With hardly any sleep, the bulk of the newsroom workers get right back to work with the daily 9 AM meeting and plans for the day ahead. Wednesday morning will see a record low for that day at six below zero. But the worst of the snow storm is over. Executive Producer Ceravolo, with two days worth of beard growth and bags under his intense eyes, sends out this e-mail:

"Great job yesterday by everyone. I drove home last night with a fuzzy feeling about News 22. I thought, man, we have some talented and hard working people who care. I knew that already, but sometimes it just slaps you in the face. Anyways, thank you all so much, especially those of you who stayed overtime, worked double shifts, came in early, etc.

Also, I know we're tired, but let's keep pushing ourselves. There's a lot of people at home tonight and they need the latest information."

It never ends in TV News.

"HEY, LOOK, HONEY, ISN'T THAT REGIS?"

Luke Choate has been a news anchor at WSBT-TV in South Bend since the mid 1980s. The dashing Choate worked with Jane Pauley earlier in his career, and has often confused for Regis ever since Regis became famous a few years ago.

CHARLIE: Luke, tell us about your connections to Jane Pauley and Regis.

LUKE: I worked with Jane Pauley at WISH-TV Indianapolis for six months. We co-anchored the Noon News. I was brought in from Flint, Michigan to co-anchor the 6PM BIG NEWS with Mike Ahern. Jane had been considered for that job but the geniuses in the front office at Corinthian Broadcasting in New York decided she wasn't ready for the 6:00 because her voice was "too abrasive."

Jane is very bright, intelligent, and funny. At that time (the early '70s) she was also very self-effacing, often belittling her abilities, her life. But when the red light came on the camera, Jane was self-assured and authoritative. In those days, she purposely emulated Barbara Walters, about the only woman then in a network anchor chair. When Jane left Indianapolis for WMAQ-TV in Chicago, Ahern and I said, "Watch out, Barbara. Jane will be replacing you on *The Today Show* in a few years." But we were wrong. Just a year later Jane was co-anchoring *The Today Show*.

The first person to tell me I looked like Regis Philbin was

my wife, Diane. One morning, before we were married, Diane was flipping through the channels, then suddenly started backtracking. She stopped on the *Regis and Kathie Lee* show on cable and said, "That guy looks just like you? Who is that?" I said, "That's Regis Philbin. He used to be the sidekick on *The Joey Bishop Show* opposite Johnny Carson years ago." I told her Regis became a household word for a few days because he practically had a nervous breakdown on the show, cried, and then resigned. Just about ruined his career.

Soon after that, their little cable show went national on syndication. *Regis and Kathie Lee Live!* was picked up by 22 WSBT. WSBT Radio personality Bob Lux was interviewing Regis on his afternoon show and mentioned that we had a news anchor that looked much like him. Regis asked Bob to send him a picture. I gave Bob a picture of Diane and me taken at Frank's Place. It wasn't long before Regis was holding that picture up on his show!

WSBT-TV (South Bend) Noon Anchor Luke "Fore" Choate and the man he is often mistaken for, Reege.

Both 22 WSBT and the staff at *Live!* kept getting calls about the resemblance, so when Regis came to South Bend to emcee the annual Moose Krause dinner my co-anchor Cindy Ward set up an interview between Regis and me. Cindy got Regis to carry on for a 90-second bit that was hilarious. He got done and said, "Cindy, is that okay?" Cindy had the segment aired on the 10:00 News that night. Regis missed it because of his emceeing, but called the newsroom from his hotel to see if it aired all right. He asked for a dub of the tape and on Monday morning his show replayed the interview for his studio audience and polled them about the likeness. Only a few saw the resemblance.

But the mistaken Regis-Luke sightings keep coming for me. Especially during football season, when folks expect to see Regis around South Bend. A kind of hush has fallen over many a restaurant in South Bend when Diane and I walk in after a Notre Dame game. Once, at popular Sunny Italy, it seemed to me that people were being really friendly, speaking to me, smiling, even gawking. I'm used to being recognized locally because my mug is on TV all the time. But this was ridiculous! Then Diane and I looked at each other and said at the same time: "It's the Regis thing!" So when two very nervous young men came over to our table we were ready. One said, "We really didn't want to bother you, sir, but aren't you Regis Philbin?" I leaned over and said, "Yeah, boys. But, you know, (pointing at Diane) this isn't Joy, is it? So let's keep this quiet, OK?" After the shock wore off, I fessed up to being a local news anchor who is often mistaken for Regis.

The mix-ups have never stopped. Some guys have been pretty embarrassed by their mistake. Notre Dame priests. Gerry Faust. And the general manager of a local TV station who will go unnamed. The funny thing about it is, I seldom know they are mistaking me for Regis because they never call me by his name. They'll say, "Hey! How are you! You're looking great!" Or, "It's really great having you here tonight." But sometimes they catch me by surprise because they really are talking to me and not mistaking me for Regis. The "Luke Sightings" are much more gratifying.

MAKING THE WORLD A BETTER PLACE

To slow everyone down in today's fast paced world, I would make everyone drive their cars in reverse in cities. It would force everyone to go slower and would keep people from using their car phones. On the freeways, people could drive forwards, but not in cities. Backwards all the way. Sure, there would be some neck stiffness from looking back all the time, but people would be forced to slow down. I don't know if it would eliminate road rage, but if anything it would change the kind of road rage that happens. People would be too busy rubbing their necks to engage in unleashed, fiery, mouth spittin' road rage.

In Spelling Bees across the world, I would not allow the use of the words "except" and "accept." I emceed a grade school spelling bee once and apparently did not properly pronounce *except*. A kid misspelled it and was eliminated from the competition. He spelled a-c-c-e-p-t. Afterwards, his mother gave me an earful. I felt like a Little League umpire.

I would require all grocery store chains to do twice-daily inspections of the little wheels on grocery carts. FACT: Every time ol' Charlie goes to the grocery store, I get a cart with a drunk little wheel. Three of the wheels are always grocery store-ready, but one always vibrates and wobbles like it has a nervous disorder. "Clack clack clack clack" it goes as I weave down aisles.

Another thing, the wheel never acts up until I'm a good fifty yards away from the sea of carts. At that point, it's too much trouble to go back.

Speaking of grocery stores, as fast as America is going these days, I really think we are going to have Cart Rage. It will be sort of a spin-off of Road Rage. Some joker will be peeling out around Aisle Four, in a hurry to get soy milk. He'll plaster a guy with a beer gut, and words will be exchanged. Cart Rage will take over, and it will be ugly. I think you'll see a case where a guy slaps another guy upside his head with a Folgers can.

I also think you'll see cart jacking as we get up around the year 2005. America will have dumbed down and morally dipped enough until it will start happening. Cart jacking will be different from car jacking in that it won't be as violent. It will simply be a case of someone coming across someone else who has shopped better. Their cart has more interesting things. The cart jacker will become envious and, if physically superior, tell them to move away from their cart, and take it and move on.

As far as movies, there are a few things I would change. My suggested changes primarily have to do with the actual viewing experience in the theater. Who hasn't had to go to the bathroom during a very good movie? I know I have. I know I hate to leave and miss a scene or two. It's not like they're going to stop the projector up there for me. I really think everyone should be able to, once a year, have the movie stopped for ninety seconds. Everyone would go into the calendar year with a Pause Pass, good for all Cinemas. Then, when you're about to burst, and the movie shows no signs of slow moments coming up (like *Out of Africa* often did), you can hold up your glow-in-the-dark Pause Pass and go, "Yo. Hold up the movie, please." Everyone else would understand. Heck, it would even allow some of them to activate their beloved pocket phones. Then you would go take care of business and get back.

At the very least, theaters could have a little port-o-let deal behind the curtain. I mean, it takes forever to leave your seat, wander out the door, and down the hall to the restroom. Nowadays, with so many of these directors making three-hour movies, something needs to be done. Whether Bush or Gore got my vote in November of 2000 depended on where they stood on this issue.

Here are some changes I suggest in the world of sports: I think football head coaches and basketball head coaches should wear uniforms during games. Baseball managers do. I think it would be amusing to watch a 58-year-old basketball coach wearing those baggy, long basketball shorts and $130 high top basketball shoes. Football head coaches would have to wear pads, cleats and a helmet. I don't know that Jimmy Johnson would have gone for the helmet during his head coaching days. He seemed pretty proud of his hair. One time, when he coached the Cowboys, he came to Notre Dame to scout the NFL prospects of the Irish. It was a low-key thing where he showed up to test them after classes. At my TV station, we got a tip that he was on campus, so we went out to interview him. No one knew exactly where he was, so we tracked him by following the cans of hair spray that were lying on the ground.

As far as hockey, I love watching it in person. I can't stand it on TV. I can't see the puck. Therefore, instead of a puck, they should use a deep frozen pork chop. Disc-like, it would sail across the ice, and would also be fun to watch when it got wrongside up and started rolling over and over. Ditch the puck. Bring on the pork chop.

Talking baseball, I think the leadoff batter should have the option of running to first *or* third base. If he hits a grounder to first, darts to third, and reaches it safely, then for the rest of the inning his team would have to score by going from third to second to first to home.

I think no hot dog should be over 75 cents. Come on! $3.75 for a dog! Hot dogs are the most overvalued things on earth. Just ahead of pre-washed jeans. And pre-washed cut off shorts.

I also think that kid baseball players on defense should stop saying, "Hey, batter, batter, hey batter, batter, SWING!" You don't hear kid basketball players say, "Hey, free throw shooter, hey, free throw shooter, MISS!" As far as T-Ball goes, if a kid whiffs at the ball more than four straight times, put him or her on a van to the library and tell them about things such as chess, math, science projects and debates. If a kid sits there and whiffs time after time at a ball that is sitting there on a tee, there is a definite hand-eye coordination problem. It probably runs in the family and cannot be helped with coaching or encouragement.

I wish ESPN2 would quit running that "crawl" non stop at the bottom of the screen. Pop the thing up twice an hour, but cease with the constant stream of information. It just keeps coming back and coming back, like the Energizer rabbit. I get sick of seeing that Zlobodon Musjovic won his first-round match in the Taiwan Tennis Open and that Vladmir Ogolf won the pole for the Baja 250. That constant crawl makes ESPN2 look like the junior varsity channel of ESPN, which I guess it is in some ways.

I would also do something about those little league parents that yell at umpires and coaches. I would require that every little league park have a Parent Penalty Box. It would be thick enough to where they could not be heard by other spectators. Any parent that mouths off at an ump or coach would be put in the Parent Penalty Box for the rest of the game. They would not be allowed to take food inside and they would have to watch *Battlefield Earth* starring John Travolta, *Ishtar* and *Autumn in New York* with Richard Gere. They would also have to take all the uniforms home afterwards and wash them. And, the League would implant a bomb chip in them. At any future game where they started jawing off at the umpire, the ump could detonate them and blow them up. There would be a "wooompf" sound. They would be imploded in a way where no nearby sane parent would be hurt. It's time for umpires to make a statement.

Speaking of Little League themes, and I'm rambling somewhat here, I would never allow a moviemaker to kill off Ashley Judd's character in the early stages of a movie. In *Simon Birch*, Ashley got konked on the head by a foul ball about a third of the way into the movie. Why in the world would any sane person want to make a movie without Ashley Judd in it from start to finish? Why didn't Ashley's character have a batting helmet on while walking from her car to the stands? Put that director in the Parent Penalty Box!

I would require that people never plant pain-in-the-rear trees in their front yards. Let me explain what a pain-in-the-rear tree is. I once had a house that appeared to have a normal, big pine tree in front. I never asked the realtor about the tree. It seemed fine. Well, a year went by and the pine needles started coming off like crazy. I'd never seen that. I always thought the needles on pine trees were there for life, like a man's need to have the remote.

I went to my neighbor, who knew everything about yards. She explained to me that it was the kind of pine tree that shed once a year. Boy, did it shed. Needles were all over the yard. It was therefore suggested that I rake the needles. I didn't warm to that idea. Raking leaves was trouble enough. Living in northern Indiana, I had always been irritated that leaves did-n't show up on trees until mid May, and then started plunging to the ground in October. That's only five months of being on limbs. Not fair.

So back to this annoying pine tree. I originally refused to rake the needles. They could just sit there and get to know the grass for all I cared. Then my neighbor told me that there was an acid in the needles that would kill the grass.

"You're kidding, aren't you?" I asked.

"No."

So, from that point on I had to rake the acid-secreting pine needles, then the stupid leaves that came shortly afterwards. As protest, I cut off the bottom five limbs of the pine tree. I often hoped for strong winds to topple it, or that I would wake up one morning and find that it had uprooted itself and left for the deep woods. Or the sea.

I would encourage everyone to wear more jump suits. Have you ever worn one? Think about it. Probably not, unless you did time in the jail, raced cars, or worked in a tire shop.

Jump suits are unbelievably comfortable. I'm not kid-ding. I recently did a TV News story on what it was like to race a stock car. Hoosier Tires provided me with a racing jump suit. I put the thing on and fell in love with it. I wore it all day at work, even when I didn't have too. I don't know about you, but I am always tucking in my dress shirt and hitching my pants. Not with a jump suit. That sucker has no middle part complications.

So, I encourage you to try a jump suit today. It could be a change in your life that would make you glad you got this book.

I would not allow SUVs to park. Have you ever tried to back out your normal-sized car next to an SUV? Those things are bigger than aircraft carriers. You back out, and back out, and you get near its back door. You still can't see if any traffic is coming, so you just say, "I give up. I can't see around this SUV. I'll just hit the gas hard in reverse and hope nobody pops me as I back out into the road!"

Therefore, SUVs should not be able to park. Anybody who operates one does so simply for a leisure drive, then it's back to their mammoth garage.

I would not allow people to say, "I know such-and-such like the back of my hand." Let's be honest. How many of us really know the back of our hands? The other day I stopped and looked at the backs of both of my hands. I was familiar with them, but I didn't *know* them like that saying insinuates. I didn't really know the directions of the veins that stick up, or the fact that there were more hairs at the base of my pinkies than anywhere else on the back of my hand. So, the next time you get ready to say that, stop and think. Do you really know the back of your hand? Have you taken the time to get to know the back of your hand? How about your Achilles tendon area? Have you spent quality time with a mirror in the bathroom getting to know your back? Both the lower base and shoulder area? Have you opened your mouth and looked under your tongue? Your belly button? Talked to it lately? Know it like you should?

BROADCASTING MEMORIES, GOOD AND ... WELL, NOT-SO-GOOD

Over 17 years of TV News broadcasting, I have spent much of my time in the newsroom guiding others, but I have also been able to get out and have some memorable experiences. Here are some that stand out. I'll start with the positive experiences and then get to the "dreaded embarrassing moments."

THE CHAMP: On Friday nights I would become a character known as "Chopper Charlie" and ride in a helicopter to cover high school football games. Every year we landed in Berrien Springs, Michigan to visit the Shamrocks football team. A couple of years ago, someone came up to me and said they worked for Muhammad Ali, who lives in Berrien Springs. They appreciated my commitment to local sports and said they could arrange for me to meet with Ali. I told them that would be great.

A few months later, our former general manager Jim Freeman told his secretary Patti Hostetler that a visit was in the works. We were given a time to come to Ali's home just outside of Berrien Springs. Patti, energetic sports reporter Mike Stack, and I made the 30 minute drive from South Bend to Ali's home with great anticipation. Patti was so excited that she about fell out of the car. I almost pulled into a drug store to get some kind of calming ointment for her.

We were just about to meet the most famous man in the world. Most people agree that Ali is better known around the globe than anybody else. When I was growing up in Mississippi, I thought the most famous person in the world was Boss

51

Hogg of "Dukes of Hazzard," but that was mainly because I never missed that show.

We pulled up to the iron gates that guard Ali's estate. We were given a code and the gates swung open and we drove in. The grounds were beautiful. Lots of open space for Ali to just get away from it all. We pulled up to the main house and an assistant came out. Super nice guy. He didn't act at all like, "Oh, brother, another arranged visit for Muhammad." He hopped in the car with us and we drove behind the house near the breakfast room. We could see Ali inside finishing up breakfast. He had a big, comfortable T-shirt on. As soon as he finished, he came outside and we followed him and his driver down to his boxing facility. He doesn't box anymore, but he had a ring put in his gym not too long ago.

His assistant introduced us to him and Ali could not have been nicer. He immediately started having fun with us. He shadowboxed Mike Stack and me. He joked with Patti, who was about to faint! I couldn't get over how easily I could understand his talking. Impressions from national TV led me to believe his Parkinson's had really slurred his speech, but I understood him fine.

He guided us around his boxing room. Pictures of championship fights from the past adorned the walls. He shared funny, inside stories while looking at several of them. Then, he had us sit down in chairs by the ring and he went into his magician act. Ali had us cracking up. He levitated for us, then did a trick where his thumb disappeared.

"What I'm about to do may get me kicked out of the Magician's Union," he said, and then showed us a fake thumb that he used to make it look like his thumb disappeared. To Mike Stack's amazement, Ali then gave him the thumb to keep. To this day, Mike has it proudly displayed in his part of the sports office.

Ali showed us how he levitated, and told us how much he enjoyed doing magic tricks. He answered any questions we had about his career, and then took us up into the ring. Patti had brought a camera, so Ali posed for pictures. He pretended to take a punch from me. He put his arm around beaming Patti. Never once did he appear to just be going through the motions.

After about 45 minutes, we said we'd better be getting back. Patti gave him a WSBT T-shirt and coffee mug. I know that had to make his year(!). He had a plane to catch to make a world appearance somewhere. He travels a ton, but Berrien Springs is home, and he has made countless appearances in southwestern Michigan and South Bend.

Notre Dame has the famous Bengal Bouts every March. Students train very hard to box to benefit the Holy Cross Missions in Bangladesh. In March of 2000, Ali made a surprise appearance to watch the boxing. He interacted with many Notre Dame students who were there watching. We had a camera there, and caught one student saying, "Oh my gosh, Muhammad Ali just shook my hand...and I'm just a freshman!!" South Bend area real estate expert Don Cressy told me that Ali went into the locker room afterwards and shook hands and signed autographs for the young men.

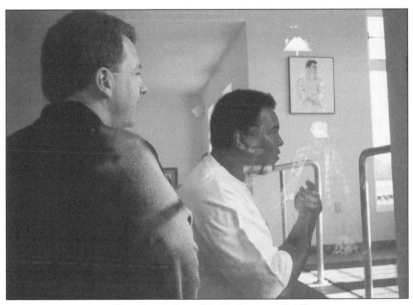

Charlie visits with Muhammad Ali
at the champ's home north of South Bend.

I wish our visit with Ali had a totally happy ending, but there is tragedy. Patti borrowed a still camera from Dennis Elsbury at WSBT to use on our Ali visit. Unfortunately, ol'

Dennis had already used the film in the camera, so all the pictures Patti took went on top of the old film, so every picture was messed up (check out my photo with Ali). I think Patti had Dennis dumped in wet concrete out back. No one has seen him at WSBT in a long time.

BILL COSBY: In 1999, the newsroom gave me the assignment of going to Chicago and interviewing Bill Cosby about the popular TV show he was hosting, *Kids Say the Darndest Things*. Photographer Ryan Flory and I drove to Lincoln Park early in the morning where they were taping the show on location. Ryan is best known for having overachieved in marriage. He married the former Julie Hail, a queen among women.

I anticipated the producers would look at us like pesky mosquitoes, but that wasn't the case at all. They went out of their way to greet us, get us set up, and assure us that Cosby would do an interview with us. We drifted towards the back of the set where it was dark and watched as they got the lighting right and everything in order to tape their show. Soon, Cosby arrived in his usual floppy sweatshirt. This one was a Loyola sweatshirt. Not two minutes after he arrived, he stepped to the middle of the set and looked around. "First of all, do we have any visitors here? Any reporters?"

That startled me, but I moved forward and acknowledged our presence.

"Come on out of the hole, man," Cosby said while moving towards me to shake my hand.

"What's your name and where are you from?" he asked as we met.

"Charlie Adams. From the CBS affiliate in South Bend, Indiana."

"All right, glad to have you," he said. Cosby looked towards the man in charge of directing the show. Cosby asked him how much longer before they started taping. The man said about ten minutes.

"I tell you what," Cosby said. "Let's do the interview you came for right now."

That really startled me. I had figured we'd be there for a couple of hours before having a chance to interview him.

Photographer Ryan quickly set up his camera and tripod as Cosby and I set down at the table where he would shortly get the kids to say darned things. As Ryan set up, Cosby and I talked college basketball. I told him about how excited Notre Dame was about freshman-to-be Matt Carroll from Philadelphia. Cosby groaned. He had wanted his beloved Temple Owls to get Carroll.

Ryan got the camera rolling and I asked Cosby about his show, and then about parenting.

"Respect. I don't care what anybody says. A husband and his wife are the parents. They are not the kids' buddies. Not their best friends. Later on in life, that description may change, but when they are growing up, the parents are not there to win the Junior Chamber of Commerce Good Guy Award, because sometimes parents try to be good guys and end up being sorry because the kid took advantage of it.

A fellow once asked me why I didn't get into trouble as a kid like getting into street fights. My answer has always been the truth and that is I didn't want to embarrass my mother and father. There certainly was peer pressure that led to me thinking I won't be one of the guys if I don't get in this fight, but by the same token it was the love and the strength my parents had that kept me from doing that stuff.

Just keep in mind. The parent is the parent."

COVERING NOTRE DAME: I have covered a boatload of Notre Dame football games over the years. In 1988, the Irish were getting ready to host bitter enemy Miami. The Hurricanes pulled into South Bend the day before the game. We went out to cover their walk-through Notre Dame Stadium. Afterwards, we interviewed head coach Jimmy Johnson. I said, "Jimmy, are you all scared Notre Dame might surprise you with more of a passing attack?"

He stared right at me and said, "Son, we are not *scared* of anything."

Well, they got beat the next day in one of the two most exciting ND games I've covered. In 1993, it was #1 vs. #2 as Florida State rolled into town. We do a live radio show before games called "GameDay SportsBeat." I interviewed O.J.

Simpson live on the field just an hour before kickoff. He was upbeat, friendly, and shaking hands with fans. Bridget Elliott of Sunny Italy (incredible Italian food!) later told me that O.J. came into their restaurant and charmed everyone. She said he went back in the kitchen and shook hands with everyone. Seven months later, there was a white Bronco chase.

I have interviewed Regis several times at Notre Dame games. He's always great. Boy, does he love Notre Dame. I have tried to interview Spike Lee at two games, but he has declined. He doesn't love Notre Dame. He rooted for Florida State at that big 1993 game and for Stanford on his next trip to South Bend. At the Stanford game, it was an honor to interview James B. Stockdale, Navy aviator, who was a prisoner of war for nearly eight years. So determined was he to avoid giving up valuable information to the enemy, he gouged his wrists with shards of glass to try to kill himself. For his country! He obviously came out alive, and is truly someone who paid the price so that we may stay a free country.

My on-field interviewing partner Bob "Muscles" Montgomery shared the microphone with me over the years. Whenever someone really cerebral was available as a guest, I gave the microphone to Bob. He has talked to "News Talk" show host Tim Russert and Gerald Ford before games. I would stand there and nod.

"Weekday SportsBeat" is a Notre Dame football tradition. If you are in South Bend for Irish games, tune into AM 960 before and after games to get outstanding coverage. It's a lot of fun to have on while you and friends are tailgating. I especially enjoy listening to Rick "Sergeant" Carter's candid assessments. He doesn't hold back with his postgame comments.

I never did see Julia Roberts when she came in for a Notre Dame-Southern Cal game with Jason Patric. Her picture is at Bruno's popular restaurant in South Bend. They stopped there to eat during their visit. In the Press Box I have bumped into the likes of Bill Bradley, Joe Montana, Rick Pitino, Al Lesar and Wayne Gretzkey. (See chapter 12 for more Notre Dame stories.)

With every memorable moment in life, there comes an embarrassing one. Here are some of my humbling stories.

PHOEBE CATES: Back in 1987 my favorite actress was Phoebe Cates. I thought she was the most beautiful person alive. She had done movies like *Gremlins* and *Fast Times at Ridgemont High*. During a visit to my hometown of Oxford, Mississippi she happened to be in town filming the eventual clunker *Heart of Dixie*. I was eating at a pizza place with my longtime friend Billy Petty when all of the sudden Phoebe and Ally Sheedy walked across the street into a health club. I almost choked on my pizza. They were staying in a nearby condo.

"Billy," I said with conviction. "I am going to go meet Phoebe Cates."

"Boy, you're crazy," Billy said. "You'll make a fool out of yourself."

I ignored him and slid out of the booth. I wished I had slapped on some of my smell-good earlier that morning. I also worried that I hadn't shaved my neck hairs in almost two weeks. I popped in the bathroom to make sure there wasn't a pepperoni on my nose or anything, took a deep breath, and walked across the parking lot to meet Phoebe.

I told myself that as soon as I walked in, she would see me, and come running to me saying, "I'm yours, forever!" The chances of that happening were slim, but it was nice to tell myself that. You should always think positive thoughts.

I got to the health club and opened the door. There she was, just ten feet from the entrance. I had assumed she would be halfway across the gym, giving me time to suavely walk across with a little steam in my stride and strike up a conversation. But no, I almost walked into her as soon as I got in the place! She looked straight at me. I had to say something right away. It was obvious I wasn't there to work out. I had no gym bag. I blurted out something about "wanting to meet you."

That went over like a lead balloon. She gave me an icy look that said, "Go back from whence thou came." I was a juvenile stalker for all she knew. Ally Sheedy was already riding a stationary bike nearby and recognized my awkwardness. She asked where I was from.

"I'm a sportscaster in Bakersfield."

Ooooooo. Another impressive comment by Adams. They're famous actresses from Hollywood, and I'm the guy that does the sports up in Bakersfield. I'm sure Phoebe entertained thoughts of leaving acclaimed actor Kevin Kline right then and there for me. She kept giving me the *depart now* look, so I backed out the door and went about my business. Ally gave me a nice smile that said, "You're not the first buffoon to approach Phoebe like this." Slumped over, I walked back into the pizza place and sat back down in the booth across from Billy.

"Did you make a fool out of yourself?" he asked without looking up.

"Yeah," I said.

"Oh, well. Eat your pizza. It's still warm."

FASHION FOLLIES: Another embarrassing moment happened to me one fall while flying around in Chopper 22 covering high school football games. This tale comes under the title of "Fashion Faux Pas." I'm not overly intelligent when it comes to clothes. I don't quite understand when you are supposed to stop wearing some clothes because of the season.

It was late October of 1998 and we had just landed in Cassopolis, Michigan to cover their game. As usual, I stood alongside the players as our photographer got highlights of the game. As I stood there, some lady kept saying, "Charlie... Charlie!!" I figured it was someone upset we didn't show more rowing highlights on the Sports, so I ignored it for awhile. Finally, after the tenth "Charlie" I turned around to see her standing at the fence motioning for me. I walked over to hear what she had to say.

She pointed at my pants, which were light cream.

"Charlie, those pants are way out of season. You can't wear light colored pants like that this time of the year. We're all up here talking about your pants."

I turned three-and-a-half shades of red and "thanked" her for her observation. I looked all over the high school football stands. Every man there either had blue jeans on or dark pants and there I was in pants that were almost white! Cassopolis was our first of three Chopper stops, so the rest of the night I tried to hide myself among the players on the sidelines. Paranoid or not, I kept imagining every fan in the stands going, "Look at that idiot in the light pants...doesn't he know it's almost November?"

Now, I only wear light colored pants in July, just to be safe.

THE MAD DASH

Part of the appeal of sportscasting for me during the years I was a sports director at WSBT-TV in South Bend was the incredible adrenaline rush of racing against the clock. There were times when I felt like James Bond trying to get to the bomb counter before it got to 0:00.

Covering Notre Dame Football meant that at least twice a season I would do "The Mad Dash" When the Irish played at Purdue and at Michigan, the games started around 2:30. Our evening newscast aired at 6:00. I knew that the games would go over three hours and not end until around 6:00. Our sportscast would air around 6:18.

Decision-makers at the station would always tell me before leaving to just worry about doing a "live shot" after the game. There wouldn't be time to feed back any interviews via satellite. Just set up outside the stadium and recap the game for the Saturday 6:00 News.

Well, there's nothing wrong with that approach, but I always wanted to push the envelope and try to get interviews on the air. Our satellite truck at Michigan is always parked outside the stadium. To get anything on air back in South Bend, I have to do the interviews on the field and then literally sprint to the truck so that we can feed by 6:15.

In 1999, Notre Dame and Michigan played a fierce game in Ann Arbor. It went down to the final minute. Time outs were called. Officials stopped the clock. Standing on the sideline, I kept glancing at my watch. It was 6:00. We had to interview players, get to the truck, edit their comments, and feed it back via satellite so that it could air for WSBT viewers at 6:20. This was going to be tricky. The game finally ended a little after six, with Michigan coming out on top in a game that had some controversial calls by the officials. Photographer Greg Carroll and I darted onto the field as soon as the final gun went off. We knew we would only have a minute or so to do interviews before the Notre Dame players trudged to their locker room. Had they won, they would have been more than happy to talk to anybody with a microphone. Having lost, all they wanted to do was shake hands with their opponents and get to the Irish locker room.

Our first target was senior receiver Bobby Brown. He had caught a key two-point conversion late in the game, but the officials felt he celebrated excessively and penalized the Irish on the kickoff. Michigan got great field position and went on to win.

We raced over to Brown to get a comment from him. He was devastated and waved us off. Other players asked us to leave him alone. My eyes cut back across the field where the Irish were shaking hands with the Wolverines. Senior defensive star Lamont Bryant was coming by me.

"Lamont, let me ask you about...."

I didn't even finish the question. His dirt and grass stained hand grabbed my shoulder and twirled me aside like I was a Pokemon toy. That was his blunt way of saying, "No comment." He pushed me fairly hard, but it didn't bother me. I remembered back earlier in the summer when Bryant had given a wonderful, inspirational talk to inner city kids on the Notre Dame campus. He was upset with the loss. I've been upset with sportscasts in the past that have gone to pot and have thrown stuff around the office. Not that either of us is right. I just understood him, I guess.

By this time, most of the team had left the field. Having been burned twice, my experience told me to seek a player who would not turn us down. I immediately thought of starting offensive lineman Jim Jones. It was his first year as a starter. He had not grown weary of the media yet. I spotted him and quickly asked him about the game. He gave an insightful answer and we thanked him.

61

I interviewed a couple of other Notre Dame players and then started the Mad Dash. It was 6:09.

"Greg, give me the tape!" Greg ejected the DVC Pro tape and I went into my Barry Sanders mode of zipping around folks on the field. Running literally as fast as I could, I blasted up the tunnel past players from both teams. At the top of the tunnel runway, I cut left and started towards the satellite truck. Thousands of fans were leaving the stadium.

"Excuse me! Coming through! Look out!"

I weaved like a water bug past fans that probably thought I was a purse-snatcher. I ran through the post game tailgaters, jumped water coolers, and hurdled fences. I bumped fans aside. Reaching the parking lot, I went into my turbo speed. All that means is that I just breathed louder, but thought in my mind that I was running faster.

Engineer Wilson Johnson stood smiling at the entrance to the truck. He always got a kick out of my mad dashes.

"You feed in two minutes," Wilson said. "I've got the station on the phone. They're all set in editing back there to take your tape feed."

Gasping for breath, I slammed the raw edit tape into the truck editing machine. I hit rewind and queued up the tape that I would edit onto as the field tape whirred backwards.

Ninety seconds to go.

I stopped the tape at the start of the Jim Jones interview. I laid down the edit and put down his interview onto the edit tape.

Sixty seconds to go.

I set the edit points of the next two interviews and laid them down. As the final edit was taking place, I picked up the phone to South Bend.

"You there, Mike?!"

Mike Stack is the popular weekend sports anchor for WSBT-TV.

"Yeah I am, Charlie," he said, "but I've got to be on set. Sports starts in a minute. Someone else will take your feed here and run it upstairs to air."

Weekend editor Jonathon Miller took the phone from Mike and told me they were rolling back in South Bend. I rewound the tape I had dubbed over the three interviews onto and told Wilson we were ready to feed.

I hit the play button and our interviews beamed back to South Bend. Mike Stack was on set and showing the highlights of the game. As soon as Jonathon had taken our fifty seconds worth of post game comments, he sprinted upstairs with the tape to the tape roller. Mike finished his highlights, listened in his earpiece to see if the tape had made it, and was told to stretch slowly by the director.

"The tape is coming, Mike."

Mike ad libbed a little about the game until he heard, "The tape is ready to go."

"Charlie Adams was on the field as the game ended just a little while ago and got these reactions from the players."

The tape rolled, aired fine, and was done.

Back in the truck, I was a sweaty mess. My work was not done though. There was much to gather for the 10:00 News. "See you in a bit, Wilson," I said as I jogged back to the locke-room to meet Greg Carroll.

He was crammed in with all the other media rolling on Coach Bob Davie's post-game comments in Michigan's pathetic excuse of a visiting locker room. After getting Davie, then it was on to try to get comments from the key players. To his credit, Bobby Brown did not duck us after the game. He felt terrible for getting flagged for excessive celebration. Personally, I felt the officials should have felt terrible for not flagging Michigan receiver David Terrell for celebrating after a catch later in the game.

We then found classy new offensive coordinator Kevin Rogers. His hand was caked with dried blood. No doubt from smacking the wall after a play that had gone awry. Still a sweaty mess, I roamed around getting comments from players until we had enough to do worthy coverage of the game.

Exhausted, Greg and I trudged back to the satellite truck where I promptly got to work putting together a lengthy story for the 10:00 Newscast. With me in the back editing away, the truck rumbled out of Ann Arbor and back towards South Bend. The whole time I was wishing it came with a shower in it!

In 1997, I tried the Mad Dash after Notre Dame's loss at Purdue. It was Purdue's first victory over the Irish in a long time, and the students went bonkers. That Mad Dash almost got quashed by us getting smashed. We got caught right in the middle of the student's celebration on the field. It was like getting caught in a hurricane. The stench of alcohol just about made me throw up. Then some student realized we were from a station in South Bend and yelled out, "Notre Dame Media!" I got popped in the head by somebody and had to bull rush my way out of there.

In 1999, my Mad Dash for Notre Dame's game at Purdue worked fine. I did have a South Bend resident named Stephanie Krizmanich tell me that she witnessed my sprint from Ross-Ade Stadium to our satellite truck parked at Mackey Arena. She said she got a big kick out of watching me run as fast as I could by a bunch of fans slowly leaving a game. I'll bet I did look like an oddball. People probably thought I was hopped up on crack cocaine, or that I was an avid Notre Dame fan who dealt with losses by running as fast as I could.

After we had wrapped up our coverage of that particular game in West Lafayette, Indiana, we rumbled back towards South Bend. We stopped at a fast food restaurant in Delphi, Indiana. Our satellite truck is plastered with *News* logos, that attracts people. Some fella came by the truck and wondered what we were doing with our TV Truck at the food joint.

"Haven't you heard?" I asked him. "Aliens are here. They're in there sucking brain waves from customers. We're beaming the story to CNN."

The man didn't know what to say to me. He bought my tall tale hook, line and sinker. It was all engineer Wilson could do to suppress his laughter.

He looked in the food joint. People seemed to be ordering food in a normal fashion, he observed.

"They don't realize they are having their brain waves sucked," I calmly stated. "The aliens are dressed as teen fast food workers. They suck as they take food orders."

"Dang..." the guy said. He had downed a few cold ones that day.

He kept looking inside the place. He looked again at our satellite truck.

"Hell, I'm going somewhere else to eat."

IF I COULD INTERVIEW
THEM AGAIN...

Here's my all-time Nice Person list from people I have covered in Sports:

Paul Mainieri (ND baseball coach), Chris Smith (Pro Golfer), Bo Carter (sports information publicist), Mike Lightfoot, Jody and Sonya Martinez (Bethel College basketball coaches), Muffet McGraw (Notre Dame women's basketball coach), Bob Davie (ND Coach), Bill Benner (former *Indianapolis Star* columnist), Luke Choate (WSBT anchor, terrible golfer), Hunter Smith (NFL punter), Tony Rice (former ND quarterback), David Haugh (*South Bend Tribune* columnist), former Purdue and Rams QB Jim Everett (he was exceptionally nice to me when I covered the Rams), LaPhonso Ellis of the NBA, soccer star Kate Sobrero, Indiana High School basketball coaches Tom DeBaets and Steve Anderson, football coaches like Tom Kurth and Chris Geesman (actually, every high school coach should be on this list), John Heisler (Notre Dame sports information director, and his staff), Boston College associate athletic director Mike Enright, former Notre Dame assistant coaches Tom McMahon, Mike Sanford, and Urban Mcyer, Pat Garrity of the NBA, the late Marv Wood (Coach Gene Hackman portrayed him loosely in *Hoosiers*), Ward Burton and Bobby Labonte (Winston Cup drivers), Glenn Carver of WREG TV sports, Peyton Manning (Indianapolis QB), Jennifer Gillom of the WNBA, Olympic gold-medalist swimmer Lindsay Benko, Van Chancellor (coach of the Houston Comets), and Digger Phelps, who has always been very nice and accessible to me.

I think the nicest and classiest coach I have ever met is Valparaiso University's Homer Drew. Impeccable character. Tremendous husband and father. Vibrant basketball mind. He is nice, successful and fulfilled. What a combo.

The nicest athlete that has ever lived has to be Archie Manning, my childhood sports hero and role model. I lived and died (died a lot) with him during his days as the Saints/Ain'ts quarterback. Growing up as a kid, I followed his every move and rooted for him despite the fact that the Saints didn't win much.

When I grew up and went into broadcasting, I got to meet him while I was covering the New Orleans Saints. We were both in LaCrosse, Wisconsin which is the sight of the Saints training camp. All of the media stay in the college dorm. The morning after meeting Archie, I trudged down the hall to the dorm's huge shower room. It had 20 spickets so that in the school year a bunch of students could shower at once. Well, I got to lathering up and in walked Archie. After saying hello to me again, and remembering my name, he started taking a shower across the room from me. We talked a little about the Saints and Ole Miss and then went our separate ways.

Later that day, I called my father in tiny Morgan City, Mississippi. He is also a huge Archie fan. I told him about meeting Archie for the first time. That excited him greatly. I was rambling along about it and said, "...and Dad, Archie and I took a shower together this morning and...."

There was silence on the other end.

"No, Dad. What I meant was we were in the same shower ROOM! It's a dorm."

There for a second, I think Dad was wondering....

In no particular order, here are my top memories of covering Notre Dame Sports since 1988.

1989 — NOTRE DAME AT MIAMI: Without at doubt, the loudest, wildest atmosphere I have ever seen for a college football game. Ask Lou Holtz. I'll bet he says the same thing. Notre Dame had a 23-game winning streak going into their game with bitter rival Miami. The Irish had knocked them off the year before in South Bend. CBS televised this game, so we did a live newscast leading up to airtime. Needless to say, we had a massive viewing audience back in South Bend.

Since the game was in decadent Miami, many of the Hurricane fans were doped up and liquored up bigtime. They were almost out of control. Notre Dame fans outside the Stadium were being pushed around. It was a little ugly. One the field, I was taken aback by the bloodthirsty look in many of the fans eyes. Man, did they want to beat Notre Dame. It was not your typical college football big game feel. It had somewhat of a big city, sins of the city of Miami feel. Miami players tried to stir up a stink with the Irish before kickoff. Holtz wouldn't let the Notre Dame players mix it up with them, which irritated Notre Dame's Ricky Watters to no end.

During our live broadcast leading up to CBS' coverage, I was all wound up on air. I was practically hollering to be heard over the crowd. I acted like I had been eating sugar cubes all afternoon. For years afterwards, I had viewers tell me they thought I was out of control. I always told them you should have been there. All I did was reflect the atmosphere, which to this day I have not seen since.

Miami won the game. Notre Dame beat them the next year and their controversial series came to a halt. I don't think Notre Dame should ever schedule them again. With so many hoodlums coming out of Miami's program, make them prove they can actually play football with student-athletes who are decent human beings before playing them again.

I do think a Notre Dame-Miami bowl game will happen someday, and that will be a hoot.

1989 — NCAA TOURNAMENT, PROVIDENCE, RHODE ISLAND, EAST REGIONAL: I was there to cover Notre Dame vs Vanderbilt, but what made the trip memorable was to be able to watch the final minutes as Princeton almost shocked mighty Georgetown and Alonzo Mourning in the first round.

I sat there fully realizing that games like this come along only every blue moon or so. I had finished my coverage of Notre Dame's win over Vanderbilt, and just sat down and admired Princeton's cuts to the baskets. The crowd knew they were watching one of the greatest upsets in NCAA Tourney history.

Princeton *had* the Hoya's, until a controversial call in the final minute gave Georgetown the momentum to hold them off. Still, it was almost surreal sitting there watching that game. I'll never forget it.

MY FAVORITE NOTRE DAME FOOTBALL PLAYER TO COVER WAS FULLBACK RODNEY CULVER. He was a gentleman. Whenever I interviewed him after practice, he always called me Mr. Adams. Not that I needed to be called that! Heck, I was 27 years old at the time. It was just the way Rodney was as a person. He would ask, "How are you, sir?" before interviews. He was aware of what I did in my job. Many Notre Dame players don't really know the local media guys from Adam. There's nothing wrong with that because they are from all over the country and tend to watch *SportsCenter* over the local stations, but Rodney was different. He seemed very genuine to me. Very intelligent and strong minded.

From what people told me, he never had an ego. He just wanted to be a real person. He was a member of the National Honor Society coming out of a very, very tough part of Detroit. He went on to become a sole captain of the 1991 Irish. Usually, Notre Dame has multiple captains, but Rodney was the only captain that Irish team needed. He went on to play for Indianapolis and San Diego in the NFL. He and fellow Domer John Carney led the Chargers Bible Study. Rodney always signed his autographs with "Mark 9:22," which states, "All things are possible to him who believes." He played a big part in the fund raising for a Child Abuse Center in San Diego.

Like everyone else, I was in disbelief when Rodney and his wife Karen died in a Florida plane crash in 1996. He was just 26. They were parents of two very young children, Briana and Jada, who were not on the plane.

After his death, I remember someone saying how the Bible says life is like a vapor. That is so true. But his memory will go on. To this day, I have covered a ton of Notre Dame football games and interviewed a bunch of players. Remember when Bob Knight said he had coached a lot of great players at IU, but his all time favorite was Pat Knight. Well, my all time favorite Notre Dame player was Rodney Culver.

18 HOLES WITH BOB DAVIE: It was a gorgeous late July morning in South Bend in the summer of 2000. I arrived at the Warren Golf Course at Notre Dame for the annual Coaches/ Media Golf Outing. The event is a symbol of the coming work crunch for the coaches. After this day of socializing, they become all-business until the clock goes 0:00 on the bowl game. As a staff they work hard all year, but from August until the national signing date in February, they work incredibly hard.

Upon dropping my golf bag off at the Ben Crenshaw-designed course, I saw where I was going to play that day with Davie. I was glad. I had known him since 1993 but had never spent four solid hours together. As someone said, you really get to know someone on the golf course.

Davie made a fine first impression on me at the 1994 Cotton Bowl. On the sidelines for the AM 960 radio show "GameDay SportsBeat," I approached the then-Texas A&M defensive coordinator about an hour and a half before kickoff. He was more than happy to do a live interview there on the field. I remember thinking to myself after the interview, "This guy is a good guy. He's going places."

Sure enough, a month later he joined Lou as Notre Dame's defensive coordinator and went on to become head coach of the Irish in 1996.

Our foursome included Davie, Lisa Nelson of Notre Dame Sports Information, Darin Pritchet of NewsTalk 960's popular "Weekday SportsBeat," and me. Athletic by nature, Davie showed a decent golf swing. You could tell he had taken the advice of golf pro's over the years and was pretty consistent. His putting touch really impressed me. As the holes went by, we talked Notre Dame football and college football in general.

"One time R.C. Slocum (the A&M Head Coach) and I were playing golf on a course with houses along the fairways," Davie said. "R.C. hit a 3-wood from the fairway and hooked it right onto the side of a nice house. WHACK! It bounced off the side. Well, he dropped another ball and hit another 3-wood. Same hook. Same direction. It hit the same house! Only this time his ball broke a window. R.C. felt awful. He walked right over to the house and knocked on the back door. After a few minutes a lady came to the door. It turns out her husband had died just about a month before that and the loud noises had really startled her. Seeing R.C. was good because then she knew no one was trying to break into her house."

"R.C. didn't know what the procedure was for hitting houses with a golf ball, but he told her he wanted to pay for damages. We learned later she was a wealthy woman. She and her late husband had never made donations to A&M, but she was so impressed with R.C. coming over and wanting to do the right thing that she ended up making a sizable donation to the University after that."

ND Coach Bob Davie with Charlie
before a round of golf in South Bend.

As our 18 holes went along, Davie got a big kick out of some of my long drives (the ones that didn't flare off into the woods). Davie shanked a short-iron approach to a green. I told him the A&M punter would do that against his Irish in September. He laughed and said the Aggies did have a new punter.

I told Davie about me being an Ole Miss grad and being excited about the Rebels' Heisman candidate Deuce McAlister.

"We almost had Deuce at Notre Dame," David said. "We recruited him hard. He wasn't that highly rated by everyone else coming out of high school, but our staff knew how great he would be. We really liked him. Great kid. Academically sound for Notre Dame. It came down to Ole Miss and us. We had him up for an official visit in January. Wouldn't you know it, it snowed like crazy and must have been twelve below zero. He ended up signing with Mississippi."

As we went along, Davie had a sparkle in his eye as he told us of his son Clay getting ready for eighth grade football and baseball. "He is into sports," Davie said. "For years, he liked playing sports, but lately the light has come on and he is really into them." Davie held up his arm and showed the bruises he sported from time spent in the backyard doing drills with his son. From going over blocking-the-plate as a catcher to tackling lessons, Davie was supportive of whatever his boy wanted to do.

A long, high ball hitter, our scramble-team used many of Davie's shots. When we got to the Longest Drive hole, Darin unleashed a powerful poke, but it sailed out of bounds.

"Tee up another one, Darin," Davie said. "Commissioner's ruling. You get another chance."

By golly, it was Bob Davie's Golf Tournament. As Commissioner, he could do such a thing! Darin fired off another one that set the standard for long drive of the day. We all agreed to keep it a secret about the "Commissioner's ruling." After reading this, please swear yourself to secrecy!

Davie knew he was coming up on a season where he was in the coaching hot seat. A 5-7 record in his third year as Irish head coach had the critics howling, but as we talked, I sensed that he had been building a strong foundation for Notre Dame Football. The 2000 season would be a doozy, but I felt if he could get through it then he would be all right. If he didn't, I knew the new coach would benefit from the foundation Davie and his staff had laid, just like Matt Doherty benefited from John MacLeod signing Troy Murphy, Matt Carroll, David Graves, Harold Swanagan and the other key basketball players.

We talked about the 2001 football season and its incredibly hard schedule.

At Nebraska. At A&M. At Purdue and Joe Tiller's offense. At Stanford. At rival Boston College. Home games against the likes of Tennessee, Southern Cal, Michigan State. If Notre Dame has big success in 2001, I will shave my head. That schedule would bring down Peyton and the Indianapolis Colts!

We got to the final three holes at Notre Dame. They are remarkable finishing holes to a first-class course. As a group we played our best golf down the stretch. I smoked some drives, Darin and Lisa put us up by the hole, and Davie nailed putts. We finished around 4:00. I had to head straight back to WSBT-TV to do the 5:30 News. Davie shook my hand and dug into his golf bag for a sleeve of golf balls. I thanked him and headed back downtown. It had been a wonderful day. Beautiful weather. Golf on one of the best courses in the Midwest. And a chance to get to know the head coach of Notre Dame better. But more importantly, I got to know Bob Davie as a person a little better.

LOU HOLTZ MEMORIES: I arrived at WSBT in the fall of 1988 as Notre Dame was marching towards the National Championship. During my first week on the air as sports anchor, Notre Dame moved to #1 in the rankings. The A.P. Poll was to be officially released at 6:30 PM on Monday. I was doing sports live outside Notre Dame practice that night at 6:20. It was my intention to meet Holtz after the 6:00 News. Well, I did sports at 6:20 and they went to the final commercials before the final segment of the News. Lo and behold, practice ended and Holtz started marching towards us. I asked Sports Information Director John Heisler if I could get Lou on live at the very end of the News and ask him about his team becoming #1 in the rankings. Heisler agreed, and went to get Lou to bring him over. I frantically told our news producer over the two-way to come back to me for the final minute of the News. I would have Holtz live to talk about the move to #1.

The producer, who shall remain nameless, wasn't interested. The producer person had come to the station from some far off place and had no idea how big ND Football was in South Bend. That person preferred to run some inane "kicker" to close the News. Something like an extra large watermelon grown in Iowa or something.

Well, Holtz walked up beside me as I was in a state of disbelief that the producer would not come back to me.

We introduced ourselves, shook hands, and he stood ready to take a question. I was hoping that the producer back in the booth would see him standing there on the monitor and come to her senses. She did not. She preferred to stick to format, so Holtz and I stared at the monitor by the field camera and watched the News end with the giant watermelon or whatever fluff they concluded with. I don't remember to be exact.

I was fit to be tied. Woooooo. I apologized to Holtz, shrugged my shoulders, and he went to answer questions from the print media. When I got back to the station I had a rather combustible talk with the young producer about her decision making....

Lou and I got along fine. He was extremely accommodating as an interview. I felt sorry for Penn State and Michigan media with all the hassles they had to go through to get regular access to Bo Schembechler and Joe Paterno. In 1989 though, Lou got "put out" with me. It was at The Kickoff Classic at Giants Stadium. Notre Dame was getting ready to play Virginia. The Irish were at the Stadium having a dinner a couple of nights before the game. I was set to go Live from the field on the 6:00 News. I went up to the banquet and asked running back Ricky Watters if he could walk over with me and be a live guest. He was glad to do it. The meal was over and they were just hanging around waiting for the team bus.

The bus was supposed to leave around 6:30, so I figured I could get Ricky on by 6:25 and he could go back up the tunnel to the bus. What I didn't expect was that sports anchor Lance "Romance" McAlister would lead with other sports news before coming to me live at Giants Stadium. I could see the Irish loading onto their bus. Finally, Lance tossed to me and I interviewed Watters. Suddenly, at the top of the tunnel, Lou appeared and stared laser holes through my skull.

"Ricky! You'd better get up here NOW! Charlie, you knew our bus was leaving!" He lit into me, and had good reason. I should have scratched the interview with Ricky and sent him back up the hill. Ricky caught some flak during his days at ND, but he was always accommodating to me, and I probably got him a little hot water that evening. Ricky went on to become the first NFL runningback to rush for 1,000 yards in a season for three different teams.

After Notre Dame whopped Virginia, I went into Lou's coaching locker room and apologized for holding up the team bus.

On the other hand, there was a time when I thought Lou was wrong. In 1993, when Notre Dame was undefeated in October, Lou saw me after practice and started raising his voice.

"I want a copy of your station's radio show from last Saturday!" He shouted loud enough to where everyone heard him. He was staring right at me. He was referring to the radio show "GameDay SportsBeat." Apparently, someone had told Lou the hosts were critical of the Irish in some areas even after Notre Dame has destroyed Southern Cal that particular weekend. I thought he was wrong to demand a tape, especially in front of everyone. I didn't do anything about getting him a tape.

Lou now does a regular column for *Blue and Gold Illustrated*, which covers Notre Dame Football in depth. It is a very insightful column in a first class publication. In an August issue, Holtz said that he believes the backlash of the NBC TV contract cost Notre Dame the 1993 National Championship. I still believe losing at home to Boston College cost them the title.

NOTRE DAME PLAYER MEMORIES: Frank Stams and Wes Pritchett of the 1988 National Champs were two of my favorites. They were nuts! We had them be guests on our Thursday night radio show at Burger King one time. Stams got up and went to the counter and announced loudly to the customers that all food would be free for the next hour. Burger King representative Bob Gorski almost keeled over from shock.

Former Irish basketball star LaPhonso Ellis was another favorite of mine. What a first class guy! He's 6' 9" or so. I'm around 6' 6". One time Notre Dame hired a professional to come in and talk to the athletes on how to deal with the media. The specialist said to make sure you look the reporter eye to eye. LaPhonso raised his hand and said, "The only one I can see eye to eye is Charlie. The others are small." LaPhonso picked Accounting as a major, which is very hard at Notre Dame. He had his struggles with his grades. At the basketball banquet his senior year, emcee Jack Lorri said, "I love LaPhonso as a person, but I'm never going to hire him as my accountant!"

In 1996 I was in Dublin, Ireland covering Notre Dame against Navy. The Notre Dame players got to Dublin and were given some free time to eat. They had their pick of all the eateries unique to Ireland. Where did most of the players go? To the Dublin Burger King.

I was impressed with how well the players carried themselves in Dublin. That's what I've always liked about covering Notre Dame. The young men are student-athletes. Sure, some get off the mark from time to time, and the media goes nuts covering those times, but the players have always impressed me in many ways.

NOTRE DAME OBSERVATIONS

Though I am now a News anchor here at WSBT-TV, I was sports director for many years at the station. I had the opportunity to cover Notre Dame sports, be around the first-class coaches and student-athletes, and witness the mystique first hand. I have watched as the Notre Dame athletic body has positioned itself to possibly become the best in overall college sports. This past year has seen remarkable success, from the national championship in women's basketball, the women's soccer team being ranked number one, the baseball team soaring to Top Five status, the men's basketball team winning a Big East championship, and on and on.

The two reasons I came to South Bend were to cover Notre Dame Football and Indiana High School Basketball. They have been two of the most tradition-rich parts of American sports. The following is a collection of my favorite thoughts, candid opinions and suggestions to make the Golden Dome sports scene even better.

Put two classy Jumbotron-type screens in the Notre Dame Stadium. The NBC timeouts are way too long. The fans deserve something to entertain them visually during those breaks. Remember, NBC stands for "Nothing But Commer-cials." This is a project long overdue.

ND should play Purdue in men's and women's basketball every season. No excuses. Get it done. Muffet's Irish play

Purdue. The ND men should also. The ND men's program should sign more players from basketball-mad Indiana.

ND Football should play a more diversified schedule. The only annual regulars on the schedule should be Michigan, Purdue, and Southern Cal. Quit playing Stanford, Michigan State, Boston College, Navy, Pitt and Air Force so much. If independent scheduling is tough, join a conference. Play more SEC schools and schedule a game vs. Memphis at Liberty Bowl Stadium. Fans would be able to have a blast in downtown Memphis at Beale St., Graceland and Mud Island.

Dan Devine should get more respect. He should have been in that book, *Notre Dame's Greatest Coaches.*

Now that Moose Krause has a statue, take his name off that lacrosse stadium near the Joyce Center. The stadium's all right, and the lacrosse program has classy people running it, but Moose deserves better than his name on a run-of-the-mill facility.

I think Notre Dame should rename Alumni Field after former men's soccer coach Mike Berticelli. He cared deeply for Notre Dame and did a fine job of fielding good teams against powerful national competition.

Notre Dame Stadium should be renamed Knute Rockne Stadium. Rockne was the most important person in the history of ND football. Without him, Notre Dame would not have become the most tradition-rich college football program in history.

A mid-sized arena should be built on campus for ND hockey, volleyball and certain women's basketball games. With the 2001 championship trophy now firmly in hand, Muffet's powerful basketball team will continue to sell out several games a year. The Joyce Center can handly the crowds for opponents like UConn, Purdue, Rutgers, Senior Day, and certain other games, but a cozier arena would provide a much better atmosphere for those mid-week games against the likes of Proficence and Virginia Tech. The smaller arena could also host certain concerts. As for the Joyce Center, those bleacher seats are awful. Fans shouldn't have to pay over $5 to sit on those uncomfortable slabs of metal.

Speaking of the Notre Dame women's basketball team, I was tickled pink to see them march to the National Championship and create so much excitement. My appreciation of women's college basketball goes back many years. I went to high school in Oxford, Mississippi with a first-class and very, very good basketball player named Jennifer Gillom. A 6' 3" incredible shooter and all-around player, Jennifer went on to become an All American at the University of Mississippi. While at Ole Miss, she was named SEC Athlete of the Year alsongside Bo Jackson. She went on to make the 1988 US women's Olympic basketball team where whe helped bring home the gold. Jennifer has been an All-Pro in the WNBA in recent years.

When I was a fellow student with Jennifer at Ole Miss, I practiced regularly against the women in their afternoon practices. Their coach, current Houston Comets Coach Van Chancellor, wanted 6' 6" guys like me at practice to play tough defense on players like Jennifer. Ole Miss was a Top Ten power in the SEC. At the time, it was common for the SEC to have seven or eight teams in the nation's Top 25. Van felt having tall guys at practice would help his Lady Rebels against the likes of Tennessee, Georgia, LSU, etc.

Basically, I got scorched regularly by Jennifer and her teammates. I would bring friends of mine to practice against them and chuckle as they got a dose of basketball humble pie. I saw first hand how skilled women's players were at the division one level. Having always loved pure basketball, I became more of a fan of the women's game than the men's game. The constant dunking in men's games bored me long ago. I liked the fundamental skills the women showed on a regular basis. They threw crisp passes, showed good shooting form, played as a team, and played with intensity all the time. Some years later, John Wooden would comment that he liked the women's game better than the men's because it was more of a true basketball style.

When I became Sports Director at WSBT-TV in South Bend in 1988 I was delighted to meet Coach Muffet McGraw. I was instantly sold on her as a person and a coach. It was easy to see that she was driven, smart, and dedicated. It was also frustrating to see very small crowds at Notre Dame women's basketball games. Fans sold out the Joyce to see the men, and packed gyms to watch Indiana High School basketball, but avoided the Joyce like the plague for women's games. Muffet kept working hard and started signing quality players. She also was constantly out doing community functions. In 1989 I was asked to go on a charity walk with her and her husband Matt. I hadn't met Matt. I would end up meeting him in a rather humiliating manner. Just before the charity walk, I was in the port-o-let doing my big job. I had forgotten to lock the door. Ol' Matt proceeded to see the VACANT sign on the outside and opened the door. There I was, sitting in all my glory.

"Uh...oh...uh...sorry," said Matt.

"Ooooops," I said, or something to that effect.

A few minutes later, Muffet asked me if I had met her husband Matt.

"Oh, yes, sure have," I said. "We met just a few minutes ago."

Year after year, Muffet fielded quality teams. I talked to people until I was blue in the face that they should watch their games, but women's college basketball fever didn't exactly sweep South Bend.

Muffet never wavered in her commitment to excellence. By the late 1990s she had built a powerhouse program that was worthy of big crowds. Then, Notre Dame Sports Marketing started doing an excellent job of promoting their games. The word got out that it was quality family entertainment and the crowds began to grow.

As I wrote in my first book, I feel that Notre Dame reaching the 1997 Final Four was the greatest accomplishment in Notre Dame Sports in the 1990s next to the women's soccer team winning it all in 1995. I said that simply because Muffet's Irish had to win at Texas in the early rounds before 10,000 hostile fans. That is very, very hard to do. Also, the Final Four was a very elite "club" at that time that seemed to feature the same teams every year. And, Notre Dame did not have great players other than Beth Morgan and Katryna Gaither.

The 1999-2000 season was very promising because Ruth Riley was a junior star. I went to Memphis to cover the Irish in the Sweet 16 against Texas Tech. Notre Dame jumped out to a 17-0 lead. I actually felt sorry for Tech and hoped they would make the game sort of close. Lo and behold, they scored 17 straight to tie it at 17. Oddest thing I had seen in years in sports. Tech went on to win as Alicia Ratay was in the Twilight Zone and not the Shooting Zone. I wanted to leave press row and tell her to "GET WITH IT AND SHOOT."

Early in this past season, I was aware how good Notre Dame was but that didn't stop me from going on "Weekday SportsBeat" and proclaiming that Notre Dame didn't have a chance against UConn in January. "UConn is unbeatable," I said. "No one can touch them." Notre Dame went on to spank them before a sold-out Joyce crowd. I kept my mouth shut after that and simply admired this very special team.

Ruth Riley is as classy as any athlete I have every cover-ed. More involved in community events than any other Notre Dame athlete, Ruth has touched thousands of lives in the South Bend area. If there was a DARE event in Starke County, Ruth was there to give a talk. National Honor Society event in Edwardsburg, Michigan? Ruth was there. Her combi-nation of work ethic, grace, humility and style was a joy to witness up close. An academic success who was a Dean's List regular, Ruth personified everything that is right about college sports.

My grandmother's maiden name was Ruth Riley. Gram, as I called her, passed away in the late 1990s. She would have been so proud to share that name with the Pride of Macy, Indiana.

This Notre Dame team had more wonderful story angles than you could imagine. Niele Ivey, the stellar point guard, was an example of perseverance, as she battled back from two knee surgeries to lead the team all the way in her fifth year of col-lege. She pushed herself to the limits of exhaustion as she rehabilitated to get her abilities back to the level it would take to lead a national championship contending team. Muffet said that she believed it was God's will that Niele make it to the

Final Four in her hometown of St. Louis as a senior because she refused to get down after the two setbacks.

Kelley Seimon was another example of class, beauty and athletic ability. Despite a hand injury that set her back in the middle of the season, Kelley showed a remarkable ability to get the ball in the basket in split second form down the stretch run of the season. Left handed or right handed, she would gobble the ball up near the basket and zap it back in a micro second. The daughter of former Minnesota Viking Jeff Siemon (who is now with Search Ministries), Kelley, when asked, shared her faith and how it had grown over the past few years. She quoted Old Testament scriptures in a *Chicago Tribune* feature about the kind of person she wanted to become and how her life was so much better when she was following Christ and doing what He wanted her to do.

The team featured every element that leads to a championship. Senior Imani Dunbar didn't play a lot, but was the consummate team player on and off the court. Karen Swanson was the Rudy-like walk on who busted her tail every day in practice. Meaghan Leahy accepted whatever playing time she got as a post player. Ratay's lethal outside shot complemented Riley's powerful inside game. Riley quit getting in foul trouble and became the best college center since Bill Walton.

Even as they battled towards the National Championship, the team was always there for the community. The WSBT-TV charity basketball team played in a charity game at Dickinson Middle School in South Bend in February. The game was held to benefit the family of a faculty member who was in very bad health. Riley, Siemon, Ivey and others game to the mid-week game upon invitation and signed autographs, held babies and humbly did anything they could to help. I was playing in the game and simply admired the way they handled themselves.

As an example of their impact, here are three things they did in November while they were preparing for the season. First, the entire team and staff took part in the first-ever "Walk for Diabetes" at University Park Mall. That same month Muffet served pancakes for the Salvation Army's "Pancake Day." Muffet also took her team (as did men's basketball coach Mike Brey) to the Logan Center to spend time with Special Olympians.

It was incredible to watch the reaction to the team as they won the National Championship. The South Bend community went bonkers over the team. They were like rock stars (classy stars, that is). To this day, fans continue to buy any kind of championship merchandise they can get their hands on (check out all the cool shirts at the new Notre Dame Bookstore!). For weeks after winning it all, Riley got stacks of fan mail every day at the Notre Dame Women's Basketball Offices. She answered every letter personally, even if it took into the night.

Season ticket packages have been selling briskly. The foundation of the program is set for future success. They have three *Parade* All-Americans coming in this season. A high school basketball star would have to be nuts not to sign with Notre Dame because of the combination of academics, athletics and uniqueness of the Notre Dame experience. They won't peel off a lot of National Championships because there are so many other top quality programs out there like the Lady Vols, UConn, Rutgers, Stanford, Vanderbilt, Purdue and so on, but they look to be Top Five every year.

There is one thing I would like to see happen to make things even better for the program and fans. It is ridiculous that ND and rival UConn don't play a home and home series EVERY season. For the 2001-2002 season, UConn does not come to South Bend because of the Big East rotating schedule. There are, oh, about 68 teams in the Big East, so every team doesn't have a home and home series with every other team. Also, Rutgers doesn't come to South Bend. Good grief.

Hello, Big East and ND! Get UConn to South Bend every year even if it's a non-conference game. Also, work to schedule series with Stanford and the Lady Vols. I'm sure it's in the works, but Tennessee hopefully will play in South Bend while the incredible Shanna Zolman of Syracuse, Indiana is playing for Tennessee.

First and foremost, the reason Notre Dame Women's Basketball has become a smash success has been the efforts of the coaches, staff and players. But, I think it's also important to give a lot of credit to Notre Dame Sports Information and Promotions. Heather Maxwell, as Marketing Promotions Coordinator for the program, did a remarkable job this past season coordinating promotions. Before her, there were people in Sports Promotions that laid the foundation to eventually connect with the community. They all deserve credit.

Bernadette "Bernie" Cafarelli did an exceptional job for years as the Sports Information contact for the team. Her professionalism in every aspect of her job helped gain widespread media crediblity for the team. Currently, Eric Wachter has the job and has continued the top quality performance in that role. By the way, Eric is the worst golfer who has ever lived.

SPORTS SUGGESTIONS AND MEDIA MUSINGS

BOB KNIGHT: I have interviewed Knight several times over the years. He always treated me in a professional manner, just like he has treated others most of the time. My theory, in my case, is that since I am 6' 6" he assumes I have played a lot of basketball and figures I know the game. I think Knight tolerates those who know something about the game better than others. Just a hunch on my part.

Like Knight, I abhor some developments in the game of basketball. The amount of traveling in the NBA, and the walking that has trickled down to the college game, makes me sick. I can't stand basketball if its not played purely. Is there a NBA player that can actually use a pivot foot without picking it up as he does a move? One time at Big Ten Media Day in Indianapolis I asked Knight about the increase in traveling. He took that question and ran with it. He explained how officials don't look at the feet enough. They look at the upper body too much.

When Florida State Coach Bobby Bowden spoke at the College Football Hall of Fame's Gridiron Legends Luncheon in June of 2000, he told the audience of over 650 these thoughts on Knight: "I'll say this about Bobby. The way he coaches, that's the way they used to coach us. It was hands on, boy. They'd didn't ask you to do something. They told you, and if you didn't they'd grab a hold of you. A writer in Fort Wayne asked me what they should do with Bobby. I said I'd love for him to coach my children. And I would, whether he's right or wrong. I don't mind someone disciplining my children. I know a lot of you don't agree with that 'cause you were raised in a different generation."

Knight's temper has made a lot of national news over the years and especially in the year 2000. David Letterman said that in coming seasons, "Everytime the opposing team scores Bobby will be given 40 milligrams of Prozac." I am often asked about his fits. I too have exploded over the years at work. I've thrown things just like he threw that chair. I have had a temper "situation" from time to time, but have mellowed over the years. I think Knight has mellowed in many areas also, but the Mt. Volcano fits still happen. To prevent mine, I took action. I saw a doctor to see if he thought I should take something. "Got any anti-temper pills there, Doc?" I did start taking Prozac, and it has helped me become a little calmer. I talked with counselors who specialize in the area of temper tantrums. I rearranged my job duties so that I didn't put myself in situations where I could have a temper fit and look like an idiot. I read and re-read the scripture in the Bible that talks about anger. "Do not be quickly provoked in your spirit, for anger resides in the lap of fools," Ecclesiastes 7:9 (NIV). I prayed about it. I started delegating more responsibilities so that I didn't put too much of a burden on myself at work. I started smelling the coffee. My "temper fits" cut down drastically to the point where I hardly ever get wound up anymore.

I think this scripture applies to Knight: "Better a patient man than a warrior. A man who controls his temper than one who takes a city." That is Proverbs 16:32 (NIV). Knight has taken cities in that he has won National Championships and Big Ten Championships, and, of course, those highly competitive IU Christmas Holiday Tournaments. But the Bible says it is a better man who controls his temper than takes a city.

It did surprise me that Knight said he wasn't going to get professional help. Not long after Knight was fired, I emceed a banquet for Boys and Girls Club, and Big Brothers/Big Sisters. College basketball announcer Dick Vitale was the speaker.

Dickie V. told me that he had told Knight that America was a forgiving nation. He had urged Knight to seek counseling and not try to justify every single controversial thing he had been involved in. If Knight would publicly say that he really needed to change a lot of his volatile behavior, America would empathize with him and support him. Heck, everybody's got problems. Knight needs to really acknowledge his temper needs professional, and more importantly, spiritual help.

Sports Spectrum magazine writer Victor Lee had this in their July-August 2000 issue: "I would like nothing more than to see a man like Knight transformed, because I know it can only happen in the truest sense by the power of Jesus Christ. The fact is, neither Bob Knight nor any other mere man can change on his own. Change comes from the transforming power of Jesus Christ working in a person's heart. If Coach Knight will turn his focus to Jesus Christ and surrender to Him, he will become a changed man, and we'll have a front-row seat to observe the work of God in the life of a man.

If he tries it any other way, he'll be gone soon enough."

THINGS I CAN'T STAND IN SPORTS: *The constant scoreboard in the corner of the screen on televised games.* Take the thing off once action starts. Put the little scoreboard up when the players are walking back to the huddle in football (not when the quarterback is throwing a bomb!), walking to the plate in baseball (not when the ball is flying towards the wall!), getting ready to shoot a free throw in basketball. I can't stand seeing the thing during actual *play*. Fox Network drives me nuts by keeping up that little scoreboard during actual NFL plays. Take it off from the point where the QB gets to the center until the tackle is made or the particular play is ended!

Another thing that drives me nuts is *trying to watch an early season NFL game being played in a stadium that also has a baseball team.* I can't watch a Miami Dolphins home game in September or October. Same with the San Diego Chargers. The football teams are on grass half the time and then cross the area that is the baseball infield! I keep thinking the cornerbacks will turn a double play. Thank goodness the 49ers don't do that anymore. I would try to watch their masterful offense at Candlestick and go "yuck" when Joe Montana and crew would get to the area where the Giants shortstop would be a few days later.

Stadiums with artificial turf are a joke. Football looks so stupid on carpet. It's not even the same game. I was so glad when places like Michigan Stadium, Giants Stadium and Arrowhead Stadium went to natural grass. Veterans Stadium is the worst stadium ever made. Three Rivers Stadium is the second worst stadium ever made. I'm sorry, but I can't take the Steelers seriously as long as they play on artificial turf. Thank goodness they're moving to a new stadium. I can't believe the people of Pennsylvania tolerate that artificial turf. Steel Curtain? Yeah, right. Not on artificial turf.

I don't like network announcers interviewing coaches and athletes at halftime. I don't think any participant should talk during an event. It's just another case of TV running the show in sports. The coach should be getting to the locker room to talk to players.

I can't stand high scoring baseball games and little dinky parks like that new Houston gizmo field. Home runs are becoming cheap in baseball, and boring like slam dunks in pro basketball.

I loved watching the Olympic hockey games — there was so much more ice to skate on. NHL rinks have the players all crammed together. Give the NHL players more room to operate. And quit expanding the NHL. There are way too many teams. I read where Montreal won't even play a game in Detroit in 2000-2001 because there are so many teams. How did Columbus get in? Somebody escort them out.

Is there anything more annoying than that "ping" sound of the aluminum bat hitting the ball in college baseball? I think any young man who has to use a metal bat loses part of his manhood. I remember covering a college baseball tournament in New Orleans. Tulane and the other teams were scoring about 24 total runs a game. It was pitiful.

Any healthy, athletic male should not be allowed to play slow pitch softball until he is 35. Be a man. Play fast pitch. Slow pitch is so easy, it's pitiful. Fast pitch is challenging. When you get to be 35, then you can play slow pitch.

I don't like local newspapers putting lots of national sports in their sports section. I go to the Web or read *USA Today* for national sports. I get a local paper for local sports. What part of L-O-C-A-L do they not understand? The *Elkhart Truth* does a great job of putting in tons of local sports. I love to read sports columnists. Opinions are a big part of sports. I would like to see at least two columns per day per local paper. The *Indianapolis Star* went to two sports columnists starting in August of 2000. David Haugh of the *South Bend Tribune* and Rick Cleveland of the Jackson (MS) *Clarion-Ledger* are among my favorite sports columnists. My favorite is Bill Benner, formerly of *The Indianapolis Star*. I flat-out love reading his work.

It has always irritated me that many people in this country label franchises like the Buffalo Bills as losers because they could not win the Super Bowl. Yeah, America does well as far as prosperity, but the emphasis on number one is out of hand. Sure, the Bills came up short in the Super Bowl game, but for several years they had a standard of excellence unmatched in the NFL. They repeatedly won their conference and reached the Super Bowl. To think of them as "losers" is asinine. If they're losers, what does that make the franchises that couldn't even get to the Super Bowl? The New York Giants beat them one year, then went pfffffttt for awhile. The Giants didn't show consistency.

Newspapers and local TV newscasts emphasize negative news too much. I feel it's one reason many people have tuned out the local news and quit reading the paper as much. I also think the public doesn't realize all the positive stories both media outlets do. Newspapers do a tremendous amount of positive features. Most TV newscasts also have uplifting and worthwhile stories, but the ratio is not 50/50. It should be 50/50. I guarantee you this country will be a better place when the ratio becomes 50/50. The problem is pride. Many journalists look at a story on someone who has a tremendous giving heart and who volunteers constantly as somewhat of a "puff" piece. They want the hard stuff. Media outlets have got to spend as much time doing stories on worthwhile, uplifting people as they do on the losers that so often grab the headlines and the lead stories. Thank goodness local TV stations are not covering "spot" crime as much. The first segments of local TV News segments were getting ridiculous with one crime story after another. The good news is that has been changing. There are many more stories of substance and community value in newscasts now than a few years ago.

Okay, I got serious there for a bit. Now back to inane issues.

If you are a hacker in golf, like me, you should look for lost balls for no longer than 30 seconds. If you can't find it, drop one and fire away. Play is slow enough without looking all over for a ball on a hole that you'll probably bogey anyway. My golf bag is full of X-out balls that my Father sends me. "Son, an x-out ball usually only has a little extra ink on the logo. It's just as good as those other expensive balls."

They also shouldn't sell mulligans at charity golf scrambles. They make the events way too long. Who cares who wins the event? The point is to support the charity and spend time getting to know others on the golf course.

PRO BASKETBALL: *I don't have a lot of respect for most NBA players.* They don't really play basketball. They're not skilled enough to make moves with a true pivot foot. Patrick Ewing is a joke. He basically runs around with the ball. When many NBA players set up for jump shots, they hop around and travel. Reggie Miller moves his feet around like crazy to get set up. I get tired of watching it. I know a lot of people in Indiana feel the same way. I love watching the teamwork and passing in the WNBA and women's college basketball. Like John Wooden, I prefer watching women's college basketball over men because it's true basketball. My favorite NBA player is Tim Duncan because he completed four years of college and has skilled low post moves. I prefer watching players that completed college, like Grant Hill. They are more intelligent and have more developed games. These mopes that come right out of high school are all flair and little substance.

The NBA seems to be more about entertainment and is moving towards pro wrasslin' type games. No wonder their ratings have been down. True sports fans want pure sports, not players palming the ball and traveling all the time. The regular season is way, way too long. That's obvious by the way some players lope up and down the court midway through the season. The season should be no more than 60 games and only 8 teams should reach the playoffs. Most of those stiffs don't belong in the playoffs anyway. What in the world is a 42-40 team doing in playoffs?!

I DIDN'T KNOW YOU WERE SO TALL!

MAJOR LEAGUE BASEBALL: *I liked it when there were just four teams in the playoffs.* Why play 162 games if you're going to let a bunch of teams in the postseason? The regular season is too long. April is too cold for baseball. Start the season about April 20th and end September 15th. Be done with the whole season by October 12th.

The only inner league baseball in the Majors should be between natural rivals. Cubs-White Sox, Yankees-Mets, Dodgers-Angels, Giants-Athletics, and a few others. Six games a season, max. No one gets excited about San Diego-Kansas City.

I detest advertising billboards on Major League outfields. They look so tacky. The Kansas City Royals' Stadium used to be so first-class. Now, all those outfield wall billboards make it look second-rate. I cannot stand the advertising behind home plate. It's seen on the most-used camera shot of baseball games: the shot from behind the pitcher into home plate. Ugh! There are even advertising signs in the dugout!

The umpires' always-changing strike zone drives me nuts. I turned off a playoff game between the Braves and Cubs a couple of years ago because I was disgusted with the strike zone they were giving Braves pitcher Tom Glavine.

There are way too many teams in the Major Leagues. Whittle some out like Montreal, Anaheim, Tampa Bay, and Kansas City so that there is better pitching throughout the league.

THE NFL: *There are too many commercials in games.* I know the NFL is getting a fortune from the networks, and the networks have to sell more commercials to make money, but enough is enough. It's ridiculous to have a team score a TD, kick the extra point, go to commercial, come back for the kickoff, and go to commercial again.

Monday Night Football has got to go with a flexible schedule, so that when teams that are expected to be good have bad seasons, they don't have to show them in December. Fans should not be stuck with pre-season tickets in their season ticket package. Ticket prices for those games should be reduced greatly. I saw where a ticket to a Chicago Bears regular season game is $37. Good grief. The Bears product is worth about $20.

90

I don't like so many players moving around because of free agency. As a fan, I like a team that keeps most of its key players for a long time. Anything less and it's not as special to follow the team. I've noticed Steelers fans become less passionate about their team. The Steel Curtain players played forever for the Steelers. Now their players come and go. I feel sorry for the passionate fans in Pennsylvania.

The NFL had better do something about the character of many of its players. There are way too many terrible off-field incidents. Many of the players had better do a better job of watching out with whom they hang out when they are socializing.

PRO ANNOUNCERS: *I want TV and radio announcers with personality and opinions.* Guys like Harry Caray. I like hearing Bob Costas' opinions. I can't stand boringly efficient, politically correct announcers.

Jack Lorri of Notre Dame Basketball is enjoyable to listen to because he will express his opinions as well as describe the game. I get a kick out of how Larry Clisby will frankly tell listeners if Purdue is playing mediocre basketball. Growing up, my favorite announcers were Jim Thacker, Bones McKinney and Billy Packer of ACC Basketball.

While I like hearing announcers with a little flair and personality, I totally agree with Augusta National for not letting Gary McCord be on CBS's Masters team. He's way too silly for The Masters. I do like the classy way CBS's Jim Nantz hosts The NCAA Tournament, *The NFL Today* and the 18th hole of The Masters. He is the best host on network TV sports.

I thought the NFL lost some credibility when Dennis Miller went on *Monday Night Football*. He says the F-word so much on other channels that I can't disassociate him from his foul mouth. Paul McGuire should be in the *Monday Night* booth. Paul Hornung would have been a good choice.

My favorite baseball announcer is Tim McCarver. On local team broadcasts, I think Hawk Harrelson of the White Sox is the best. I miss Joe Garigiola and Tony Kubek. I think the best NFL sportscaster is ESPN's Mark Malone. He has worked so hard on becoming a professional that I don't even think of him as the former Steelers QB.

I think *ESPN SportsCenter* has become way too irreverent. Bob Costas once said that too many of their anchors act like they're auditioning for the local comedy club. Bob Ley seems to be the only one there who takes anything seriously. *SportsCenter* has succeeded in making the regular season of pro sports somewhat of a joke.

As far as local TV sportscasters go, Michael Rubenstein was about the best I've seen in running a sports department that daily churned out good local stories. He was the longtime Sports director at WLBT-TV in Jackson, Mississippi before leaving to spearhead the move to build the Mississippi Sports Hall of Fame. Every sportscast had a feature with depth to it. Rubenstein and his staff were always on top of stories, and were committed to local. His reporters were always top notch. My favorite was Ed Fiddler. His packages were a treat to watch. Well written. Energetic. Fiddler knew how to put a piece together.

I think Jim Henderson of WWL-TV is probably the most professional local TV sports anchor in the business. He heads up a first class operation at the CBS affiliate in New Orleans. A first class writer with a literary background, Henderson also has a razor sharp wit. Back in the early '90s, Saints general manager Jim Finks had to go in the hospital for some tests on his heart. Finks was a tough negotiator with players. He was a stern businessman. When he got out of the hospital and had a press conference to talk about things, Henderson was in attendance. Finks was explaining what the doctors had done to his heart when Henderson gently interrupted him.

"Did they find a heart?" asked Henderson.

The media room roared with laughter.

With a sly smile, Finks looked back at Henderson.

"A heart of stone. They found a heart of stone!"

THE COLLEGE FOOTBALL
HALL OF FAME

The world-class facility opened in 1995 in downtown South Bend. In the midst of charming shops, the famous South Bend Chocolate Café, the delicious custard of Scoops, and the big city atmosphere of The Vine restaurant, the Hall is a remarkable structure.

It has been my privilege to be involved in their Enshrinement ceremonies each August and their popular Gridiron Legends Luncheons. In no particular order, here are my most special memories of things that have happened at the Hall since it came to South Bend.

1999 — FORMER SAN DIEGO STATE COACH DON "AIR" CORYELL ADMITTING HIS DYSLEXIA PUBLICLY FOR THE FIRST TIME: Often breaking down during his enshrinement speech, Coryell said he spoke with a lisp as a child, stuttered, and could not spell or read. He said football finally game him the confidence he severely lacked as a youngster and gave him a tremendous amount of opportunities. "I wasn't the dumb kid in school who talked funny," he said. "Football gave me confidence."

Coryell got a standing ovation. 5:30 local TV News Anchor Amanda Hart was brought to tears at her table. I felt fortunate to be there and came away inspired with how he carried himself during his talk.

WALTER PAYTON AND TERRY BRADSHAW BEING EN-SHRINED IN 1996: Payton gave a riveting talk that emphasized to young people that they could reach their dreams. His talk was so sincere. He spoke from experience, that's for sure. He talked with dignity and class. So healthy looking, none of us had any idea he was just a few years away from passing away. But Walter got the most out of every second of life. I remember reading how he used to cut up at Bears offices by sometimes answering the main phone. Fans never had any idea that Walter had answered the phone. His zest for life was seen first hand by Kent Stephens, collections manager of the Hall of Fame.

"The memory that most of us have of Walter from that weekend was how much fun he was having while the rest of us were all so serious, due to the fact that this was just our second Enshrinement festival. While we were trying to get everyone to autograph all of our memorabilia, get them in sports coats, and line them up to go out to the gridiron, Walter was joking around to the point where a few of us were getting a bit exasperated. When I tried to get him to autograph a couple of extra items, he looked at me and then tweaked my nipple! I didn't know what to do or so and just sort of stood there. After he signed all of the items, Julie Lang tried to get Walter in his sport coat and lined up. He was all over the room, visiting and joking with the other inductees. Finally, Julie looked to Coach Eddie Robinson to help her out.

'Eddie, please tell Walter to listen and do what he is told,' said Julie.

'Well, I don't know why he will listen to me now,' the Grambling Coach said. 'He never listened to me when I was coaching against him.'

In any event, everything came off fine, and I guess we should have known that a pro like Payton would be ready when we really needed him."

Terry Bradshaw was a hoot that afternoon! Enshrined for his blonde bomber quarterbacking at Louisiana Tech, Bradshaw waved his arms all over and shouted, "I LUU-UVVVVV college fooootballlllllll."

Hedge "bundle of energy" Harridge used to be in public relations with the Hall. She always hit it off with the Hall of Famers. Here are her memories of Bradshaw.

"We had asked the Moose Krause Club guys to escort the Hall of Famers to the podium on Enshrinement Day. We were worried they (not Joe Doyle and Bob Nagle) would get mobbed by the fans. Bradshaw told me over the phone that he didn't want a bodyguard, so to speak. He said, 'Hedge, I want a little old lady, kind of crabby, like you, Hedge!'

So, on Enshrinement Day, I was waiting with him and Walter Payton on the ramp. A fan was leaning over the railing with a country music album Bradshaw recorded years ago when he had a full head of hair. Terry saw the album and said, 'That was the only copy that sold!'

A lot of people thought Bradshaw wasn't cooperative with the fans, but I thought he was great with them. He did have to leave after the ceremony but he was nice to the fans when I was around him."

Hedge remembers the year former Notre Dame tight end Ken MacAfee was enshrined in the Hall.

"I was with Ken to do an early morning TV interview with a South Bend station. I was holding one of his Notre Dame helmets, which was autographed. It flipped out of my hand and fell on my feet and broke some of my toes! Ken is a dentist. He wrapped my feet for me there and helped me get treatment."

Hedge became especially close with many of Notre Dame's greatest players.

"Angelo Bertelli, Jack Connor, Jerry Groom and others flew me from South Bend to New York for the Heisman Dinner one year. They wanted to do something nice for me. I sat next to Yogi Berra. We told jokes to each other all night!

One year, when we were having a big Notre Dame-Army Banquet at the Hall, I was talking with Johnny Lujack. Earlier, I had met Sister 'Shorty' of Notre Dame, who had always had a big crush on Lujack. Jim O'Connor of the Notre Dame bookstore knew this and brought Sister Shorty to the Hall to meet Lujack. Angelo Bertelli was there and told Lujack to give her a kiss or God would strike him down.

I introduced Sister Shorty, who is less than five feet tall, to Lujack. She told him she had always had a crush on him. Lujack kissed her on her cheek.

'God will strike you dead now,' Bertelli roared.

'I've got to go to confession!' Lujack said.

Sister Shorty told him that if he had married her she never would have become a nun. As she left, she looked up and said, 'God, don't take me now. I'm already in heaven!' "

HERSCHEL WALKER'S ACCEPTANCE SPEECH IN 2000: The Player of the Decade of the '80s stepped to the podium and looked out at the large crowd on hand for the Enshrinement Banquet. At age 38, he looked in super shape. Because of his discipline in life, it's doubtful the former Georgia Bulldog will ever be out of great shape.

"First, I must acknowledge my Lord and Savior Jesus Christ," Herschel said. "It is written that if you do not acknowledge him, he will not acknowledge you before the Father."

Herschel has always been known for his positive, upbeat, sincere and humble attitudes.

"I want to share a story with you about two kids," Herschel said. "A father had a very negative boy and a very positive boy. For the negative little boy, the father got him a room full of the best toys. For the positive kid, the father got him a room full of horse manure. The positive kid saw the manure and started shoveling right away. He was upbeat all the time. Meanwhile, the negative kid started complaining about the colors of the toys and how he wanted different toys. The father watched the positive boy smile as he shoveled manure over his shoulder and out of the room. The father couldn't believe how happy the kid was, so he asked him why he was so positive.

The boy said, 'Well, as much horse manure is in this room, there must be a pony at the bottom of it.' "

Everyone laughed. Herschel flashed that famous smile of his. He went on to talk about the importance of being positive.

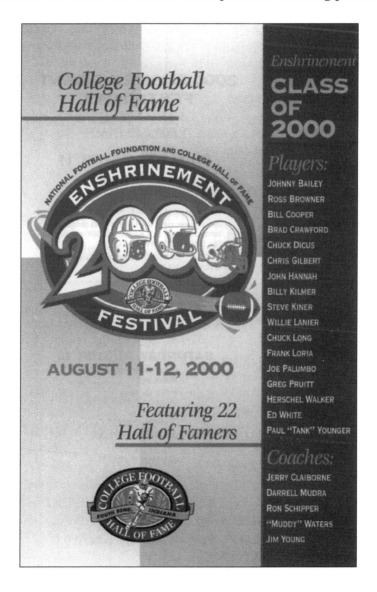

"Jesus promised us greatness, but we can't get to it unless we quit looking and focusing on the manure of life. Jesus loves you all. Thank you. Good night."

Later that evening, Herschel stopped by the popular restaurant The Vine, which is right next to the Hall. It is alongside the famous South Bend Chocolate Café with its chocolate covered strawberries. Herschel had people coming up to him for two hours. He signed autographs, posed for pictures, and was a hit with everyone that night.

Fans come into South Bend from all over the country for Enshrinement Weekend. Cody Wilson flew all the way from Fresno, California to watch Herschel go into The Hall. Wilson happened to see Herschel going back to his hotel and ran up to him. Herschel stopped, shook his hand, and talked with him there by the street.

THE FLAG FOOTBALL GAMES: They happen on the gridiron right in front of the Hall at each Enshrinement festival. My favorite memory is former BYU quarterback Jim McMahon making the game winning interception at the 1999 game as his West squad beat the East 30-22. Former Nebraska Coach Tom Osborne coached the East. McMahon was sharp at QB, but it was his interception in overtime as a Safety that secured the victory for his side. McMahon was MVP of the game. He was 7-12 passing for 70 yards and three touchdowns.

The 1998 game had Eddie Robinson as the coach of the victorious East. Eddie won his "409th" college game. Notre Dame's Ken McAfee led the game in tackles.

The 2000 flag football game featured the feathery passing touch of former UCLA and Redskins star Billy Kilmer. Wearing a baseball cap, he also was the nose guard on defense! His pass rush was not exactly like a rampaging bull.

I cannot wait to see John Elway, Dan Dierdorf and Marcus Allen in the 2001 game, and QB's like Steve Young and Dan Marino in near-future games. Jerry Rice will be a receiver. Lou Holtz will coach one of the fun-filled games. The Flag Football games are a blast for the fans that get to sit right next to the field.

"Sometimes the Enshrinees are not very enthusiastic about playing in the game," said Stephens. "But once the game gets started, they are out there playing as if they were still in college. There are guys in their 50s and 60s who will still dive for loose balls and do anything to throw a block."

THE ENSHRINEE'S PRESS CONFERENCE: This happens during Enshrinement Weekend each August. It is unique in that the fans can go to the press conference. The Hall of Famers are given matching shirts and seated at a two-tier podium. The fans and media are seated throughout the spacious banquet room. Portraits of all the Heisman winners line the walls behind the Hall of Famers.

The Hall of Famers talk about football and about life. Remarkable stories are shared over the 90 minutes or so. Former UCLA and Redskins star Billy Kilmer talked about his daughter, Cathy, who has cerebral palsy. She cannot walk. Kilmer shared how Cathy graduated from high school and junior college never having gotten out of a wheel chair. She was the one who lifted Kilmer's spirits when he had a bad car accident after college.

"I think of her all the time and, if things are bad, I think I never had it so good," said Kilmer, to a packed room.

THE KEY BANK COLLEGE FOOTBALL HALL OF FAME GRIDIRON LEGEND LUNCHEON SERIES: One of the traditions is to get the National Championship coach in to speak at one of the popular luncheons. Florida State's Bobby Bowden made people laugh so much during his June 2000 talk that their mouths hurt afterwards.

On growing up in the Depression: "I had aunts, uncles and cousins who lost jobs and moved in with us. My Granddad slept in my bed with me until I was 15. Four cousins slept in the bed next to mine. I never slept alone until I got married!"

On flying up to South Bend to speak at the luncheon: "I said to my wife Ann, 'I've got to go to South Bend to see the College Football Hall of Fame. I'm trying to get in that place one of these days.' She said, 'yeah, you love football more than you do me.'

'I said, college or pro?' "

On going through the Hall for the first time: "Boy, that was exciting. Bernie Kish took me in there where you think you're in Michigan Stadium. Boy, I got so fired up...man, I wanted to go get my coaching hat and my whistle!!"

On his #1 Seminoles losing to #2 Notre Dame in their 1993 showdown in South Bend: "Boy, that was the wildest place I've ever been in my life. Notre Dame beat us, but got beat the next week by Boston College. Notre Dame probably was the best football team in the country that year, but I ain't giving Lou that trophy back!"

On knowing Lou Holtz for a long time: "I've known Lou since he started coaching. Lou's Catholic. I'm Southern Baptist. We got Southern Baptists down there were we live. Ya'll ought to try it. It ain't bad. I said to Lou one time, 'Knute Rockne has been a hero to me. I'd give anything to have met him. I said, in fact, when I die and go to Heaven, I'm gonna look up coach Rockne and tell him I admire him.'

You know Lou, always cynical. He said, 'What if he's not in Heaven?'

I said, 'Well, how 'bout you telling him?' "

On Notre Dame Football: "I was raised in Birmingham, Alabama. Growing up, I kept up with Auburn and Alabama and Notre Dame. They broadcast Notre Dame games in Birmingham. Why, I don't know — to a bunch of Southern Baptists. I guess it was them dadgum Methodists that brought them in there. My first hero from Notre Dame was Angelo Bertelli, Notre Dame's first Heisman. I met him in New York ten years ago and was thrilled. Three years ago, they let me join Leahy's Lads. They picked me as Coach of the Year. Buddy, you think I wasn't excited about that!! On my desk I have just two trophies. Frank Leahy and Bob Neyland.

To me, Notre Dame does it right. There are a lot of people who are successful, but do it wrong." [He listed the likes of Howard Stern, Al Capone, and Larry Flynt.]

"Ara was one of my favorites. I met him in 1963 when he was at Northwestern. I always thought he was one of the brilliant coaches — smart enough to get out when he was young."

Former Notre Dame Heisman winner and Packers star Paul

Hornung entertained a large crowd during his luncheon talk in July of 2000. Here are some of the nuggets Hornung shared with the fans.

"A lot of people don't know I played basketball at Notre Dame. I played as a sophomore. Football Coach Terry Brennan talked me out of playing my junior year. IIc didn't want me to fall behind in my studies.

I feel very fortunate to have played for both the Irish and the Packers. *Sports Illustrated* did a poll on the top places to watch football. Notre Dame was number one in college. Lambeau Field was number one in the NFL.

As the number one pick of the 1956 NFL Draft I got a salary of $15,000 and a signing bonus of $3,500. Last year, the number one NFL pick got $78 million.

George Halas is the #1 name in the history of the NFL. No question.

Charlie interviewed former ND Heisman winner Paul Hornung at the College Football Hall of Fame.

Dick Butkus is the toughest linebacker to ever play, bar none. He told me once he never lifted any weights. He was 260 pounds. He told me if he lifted he would be 320...and quicker! I told him he would be barred from the NFL.

The most definitive book on Vince Lombardi is *When Pride Still Mattered.*"

Hornung raved about that book and the influence Lombardi had on his life. When asked about the state of Notre Dame football, he remarked about a *Sports Illustrated* article that said all Notre Dame players have to take Calculus.

"Thank God I didn't have to take Calculus. It's ridiculous that the players have to take that. That's for people who study engineering. I'm not talking about lowering standards...."

Peyton Manning was scheduled as a speaker for the 2001 Luncheon Series, and also to address the Notre Dame School of Business. Peyton graduated in just three years at Tennessee.

Bo Schembechler, Mike Ditka, Bowden and Paul Hornung were big hits in 2000. People still discuss talks by the likes of Danny White, Lloyd Carr, Eddie Robinson and Joe Theismann. Lou Holtz, ABC's Keith Jackson, Tom Osborne, and Wille Lanier were among the other speakers for 2001.

THE VOLUNTEERS AT THE HALL: I love being around the volunteers. They are so dedicated and important to the Hall's daily operations. They also have some great stories. Don Steinhilber told me the story of a slow pitch softball game he went to in South Bend back in the summer of 1978:

"My wife Helen and I wanted to go see Bob Schell, who was on Clay High's 1970 State Championship Baseball team. He went on to play in the Cubs organization. Bob's father Jim was our neighbor. Jim told us of a slow pitch state tournament game at Boland Park on a Sunday morning. Word that Joe Montana was on Bob Schell's team increased our interest and off we went.

When we arrived at the park, we found very few fans despite reports of large crowds at previous games. This game had been set back from Saturday because of Bob Schell's wedding and the rescheduling obviously affected attendance.

The game had O.J. Shoemaker of South Bend facing Carpet Center 500 Platolene of Terre Haute. As we expected, Montana and Schell played for Shoemaker. We were very surprised and, of course, elated to see that Larry Bird was in the Carpet Center lineup. Montana and Bird were on the verge of their historic senior seasons at Notre Dame and Indiana State. Both of them did okay in the field. Offensively, neither got a hit. I do remember Joe Montana showing his aggressiveness by scoring from second on a sacrifice fly. There were very few fans there. Nobody went after autographs.

Bird's Terre Haute team went on to win the state 12-inch championship that weekend in South Bend. Bird hit six home runs in the tournament to share most home run honors with Shoemaker pitcher Larry Trzaskowski. Bird's team beat Shipshewana Auction 9-8 in the championship game. Montana's team finished in third place.

It's funny. I went to see a slow pitch softball game, and got a memory out of it. Two men who rose to the very top of their professional sports playing against each other on a lazy summer day in South Bend."

BRETT EASTBURN

In seventeen years of local TV News, I have done thousands of stories. None of the subjects stand out like Brett Eastburn.

In 1998, I was walking by the Assignment Desk in the newsroom at WSBT-TV when I saw a flyer about a man that was going to give a motivational talk that day. The man, it read, had no arms and no legs but did not consider himself handicapped.

"That seems handicapped to me," I thought to myself.

I asked Assignment Desk operator Big John Snyder if I could cover the story. He thought it was a great idea and sent photographer Brian O'Donnell with me to the local middle school that Eastburn was talking at that afternoon.

The room must have had 60 students in it. They were all healthy and active. They chatted away, but when Brett whirred into the room on his wheelchair, they took notice! He went on to fire everyone in the room up.

"The definition of a handicap is that it's a thing, not a person," he said. "God made me this way for a reason, and that reason is to help others."

Brett's remarkable life has seen him become a top-flight wrestler. He has taken up archery. He showed the kids how he can play basketball, and threw a football out to them. He popped the top off a marker, and using his mouth drew a picture of Garfield that drew "ooooooohs" when he showed it.

"I believe this country has a big problem with three strikes and you're out," Eastburn said. "People usually try something

Dynamic motivational speaker, Brett Eastburn.

three times and they quit. I haven't quit trying. It took me over 50 times before I could turn a doorknob. I learned that it takes three points of pressure to turn one. The curve at the end of my right arm has two points of pressure. My little left arm has the third point of pressure."

105

Eastburn has talked before thousands of people. He has changed attitudes in a big way. Not long ago he was scheduled to speak at a high school. A teacher there had been in a car accident. His wife had died. He broke his jaw. His hobby was playing the trumpet. His whole life was in shambles. He had been so depressed that he was going to open the gym that day for Brett's program. That was going to be the last thing he ever did. He was going to commit suicide. But he saw the program and changed his mind.

A few years ago Eastburn talked in Japan. Handicapped children there are often put into special schools. "I told those kids through an interpreter that the only way they'd be in the normal school system was to fight," Eastburn said. "Months later, three sued the school system to get in."

Thanks to the St. Joseph County Humane Society and Midwest Assistance Dogs Program, Brett has Murray the dog to help him with things like fetching a soda from the fridge. "They got him from the pound," Eastburn said. "That's what's really great about it. He does a lot of things."

Brett got married in the summer of 2000 to Chrissa, who is a wonderful person. At their wedding in North Liberty, Indiana, Murray the dog had a specially fitted tux on as he came down the aisle with Brett.

The minister tickled everyone there when he told Brett that sometimes women spend a long time getting a man to the altar, and then spend the rest of their lives trying to alter him. He was kidding.

I think.

The ceremony was beautiful. With no arms, Brett was given Chrissa's ring and put it on her finger with his mouth. Obviously, Brett cannot wear a ring, so Chrissa put his ring on his ear lobe.

Together, Brett and Chrissa run his Motivational Speaker business. Brett gives talks to students of all ages, businesses, camps, retreats, churches and civic groups. They can be reached at 219-784-5677.

THE INTIMIDATOR: NASCAR'S LAST AMERICAN COWBOY

The night before I left South Bend to cover Speedweek 2001 at Daytona for WSBT-TV, I called my father in Mississippi. He's not a NASCAR fan. He's more of a college football and college basketball fan, but he was going to keep up with the Daytona 500 since I would be there covering it. I told him the key to becoming a race fan was picking a driver and rooting for him.

"Follow Dale Earnhardt, Sr.," I told him. "He's a throwback to NASCAR's past who can still whip the young drivers of today."

He told me he would watch the whole race and cheer for the black #3 car.

At Daytona, photographer John Rabold and I roamed the garage area interviewing many drivers during the week. Our emphasis for much of the week was on South Bend LaSalle High grad Ryan Newman, an up and coming driver destined for success in Winston Cup one day very soon. Roger Penske had signed him to be teammates with Rusty Wallace and Jeremy Mayfield. Ryan was to run three different circuits of racing this season before going Winston Cup full time. Everyone I interviewed, from A.J. Foyt to Jeff Gordon, Tony Stewart, Rusty Wallace, Buddy Baker, Benny Parsons and other big names raved about the South Bend kid's ability to handle and know a car, and his intelligence from pursuing an engineering degree from Purdue. Newman had won the ARCA race at Daytona the week before the 500. It was his first race at Daytona and he won it! His racing coach, Buddy Baker, told me that Ryan had four people talking in his ear during the late stages. Team owner Roger Penske, Baker and others were giving him advice. He listened politely and then made his own correct call that won the race with a late-stage pass.

While seeking interviews we never ran into Earnhardt. He didn't go out of his way to make himself available for the media. Last year, right after the Brickyard 400, my photographer Jade Birch and I had to stride briskly sideways to interview Earnhardt as he rushed to his RV. A news crew from Indianapolis beside us smacked right into a fuel pump and fell down as Dale kept going to get out of Gasoline Alley. He did everything hard. You'd better be ready if you were around him.

Wednesday was Valentine's Day. We did a story on a couple that got married in Victory Lane that day as cars rumbled around the Speedway. When told that most women wouldn't want to be married in Victory Lane, the bride said, "I'm not every woman." About 20 couples a year get married in Victory Lane. That night on the 5:30 News I ran an interview clip with Earnhardt talking about what he gets his wife Teresa for Valentine's. He talked about how flowers are always good. Chocolate. Teddy bears. He then said he liked most to work on surprise gifts for her. He loved to get her a gift that caught her off guard. He said it was tough to surprise her, but he usually got it done.

A couple of nights before the 500 at Daytona, we were in Victory Lane doing live reports back to News 22. Practice had ended for the day, but out of the darkness came the Pace Car roaring around the Speedway. It was Earnhardt giving Terry Bradshaw a high speed tour of the raceway. We all watched as Earnhardt steered the car into the grass at the finish line and cut donuts. I chuckled as I wondered how loud Bradshaw was laughing inside that car.

Late in the week, a group of fans from South Bend, Plymouth and Fort Wayne, Indiana invited us to come by their hotel on Daytona Beach for their annual cookout. Over 40 folks were there, including South Bend Motor Speedway Owner Mike Bird, his daughter Amy Steigmeyer, Tom Isch and their super steak cooker, Mark Aker. All the folks from Plymouth were still excited over their Pilgrims beating arch rival Warsaw in basketball a few days before Speedweek. They were all talking about Plymouth eighth-grader Kyle Benge and his already-legendary basketball skills.

We sat around and talked racing into the night. You could go up and down Daytona Beach and find numerous cookouts with fans excited about the race and how their favorite driver would do. It really hit me then about how much of a family thing racing is. Race fans are good people who know how to have a good time.

On the Friday before the Daytona 500, photographer John Rabold and I roamed the infield to do features on the pulse of NASCAR, the fans. We came across a black school bus painted and designed in honor of Dale Earnhardt. We interviewed the owner, Miloy Kelley, of Florida. He gushed with pride about his allegiance to The Intimidator. He talked about how much Dale loved his little girl, his wife Teresa, and how much closer he was getting to his son, Dale, Jr. Miloy went on and on about Earnhardt being the last American cowboy in NASCAR. He took me around his school bus and showed me the sign on front that read "Earnhardt Express." The word "Intimidator" was painted on the side.

"People either love us or hate us on the road," he said. "They either cheer the bus or give us the ol' number one sign."

An Earnhardt fan nearby showed us the alligator tail they were cooking that night. Sure enough, we later tried some. It was good, though I don't think LaSalle Grill in downtown South Bend will be putting it on the menu.

The IROC race on Friday made news when erratic driving Eddie Cheever, Jr. bumped Earnhardt out of contention late in the race. In his style, Earnhardt roared after him and bumped Cheever's car out of control after the race. I remember marvelling at how loud the cheer was for Earnhardt's "payback." Make no mistake about it. Earnhardt had the most fans in NASCAR, and they loved his hard-charging ways.

Ironic or not, the local Daytona paper had a large headline the next day that read "Dale Nailed" on the front page.

Saturday's NASCAR Busch Race found us focusing on LaPorte's Tony Raines, who was in the Bayer Chevrolet. We did an in-depth feature on what it's like before, during and after a race at Daytona. We followed Tony's wife Susan, who is an Elkhart native, to chapel where she prayed for her husband's safety. Crew member Shorty, who drives the car in a truck from race to race, was there praying with her. We watched just before the Busch race as a chaplain went to Tony, laid his hand on his shoulder, and they prayed beside his race car. During the race, photographer Rabold and I stayed in the pits. Raines started in the back of the pack because of a frustrating week of practice and qualifying, but roared up to 12th in the late stages when Susan handed me a note from her position up high next to the crew chief.

"The shock is broken in Tony's car," it read.

I looked up at her. Serious concern was etched in her face.

As Tony's car sped at 180 miles per hour, the broken shock started eating away at the tires. Tony wanted to come in. His crew told him to stay out. There were just 20 laps to go. They wanted him to try to finish. The car became harder and harder to control. In a split seconds time, Tony was bumped from behind and went flying up into the air. If not for special flaps inserted on the roof, he would have joined the Space Shuttle. It was the most spectacular crash of Speedweek up until that point.

In the pits everyone scrambled. In the haste to get a reaction shot, photographer Rabold tripped over a tire jack and fell to the asphalt, cutting his knee. He limped, and I walked over to Tony's garage, where his battered Chevrolet was brought. I asked Tony what it was like to be in such a crash, where your car flies up into the air.

"It gets real quiet," he said as sweat poured down his face. "Normally, it's so loud in a car as you race around, but when you go up in the air, it gets real quiet. It's like an amusement ride."

We stepped back as Tony stayed in the car and stared straight ahead for the longest time. He wasn't thinking about the horrific crash. He was upset they hadn't finished the race and how much that would hurt in the points standings. Dancing with death is something these guys just don't dwell on a lot.

Race day on Sunday for the 500 was gorgeous. Ninety minutes before the race, we watched as fans were allowed onto the speedway where they signed their name on the finish line. Most fans scribbled something about #3. Rabold and I went over to the garage area where the drivers were inside a building having the pre-race meeting. From what I was told, Earnhardt was sitting up front and center. A horde of fans waited outside hoping to get a glimpse of the drivers as they left the building. We watched as Earnhardt was introduced for the final time. The roar was far above that any other driver got as he waved to the crowd while walking up on an infield stage. Just before the race, he kissed his wife Teresa for what appeared to many to be a longer good luck embrace than most "before the race" hugs.

I stood at Earnhardt's pit during much of the race. I looked inside his car as he rumbled in for a pit stop and saw the face of a man dead-set on going all out that day. He stared straight ahead as they changed his tires and refueled his black Monte Carlo, and he was off again. It would be his final pit stop.

I went up in the tower by the finish line to watch much of the final parts of the race. I was back down at the finish line when the final lap arrived. I watched as Earnhardt crashed, and then I focused on Michael Waltrip's dash to beat Dale, Jr. Like everyone else, I figured The Intimidator would crawl out of his car, maybe smack Ken Schrader, and hustle to Victory Lane to congratulate Waltrip and his son. Heck, this was a guy who once jumped out of an ambulance after a crash to get back in his race car when he learned it was still driveable.

I first sensed something was wrong when we went to Earnhardt's garage to get reaction on how he was doing. His crew members, strong, hard men like their boss, were visibly shaken. A security guard got in our face and kept saying, "There is no story here. Do you hear me? There is no story here."

I was in Victory Lane getting ready to do a live report for the 6 PM News when word started to get around. I learned that his condition was serious and that he had been knocked unconcious. Then I got confirmation it was critical. A veteran broadcast journalist told me his sources told him Earnhardt was bleeding from the ears and mouth. I found myself thinking, "Dale Earnhardt can't die...he's Dale Earnhardt." But my journalistic instincts told me that he was gone.

After several mad dashes between my live shot location and the Media Room, I got confirmation on the death and we reported it in the 6:00 News. We were later told WSBT reported the news ten minutes before ESPN and CNN. We ended the newscast and photographer Rabold and I headed into the infield of Daytona Speedway where distraught Earnhardt fans were crying, staring into the darkness with disbelief, and wearing expressions of shock on their face. It was tough, but we had to get coverage for the 11:00 News that night.

Bob Pawlik, a fan from Niles, Michigan, told us that, "It was the saddest day in the history of NASCAR." One man said he was so confused that he didn't know what to do. We then went to find Miloy Kelley, the proudest Earnhardt fan of them all. Outside his black school bus with the huge # 3 on the side, his friends stood around a fire. I asked about Miloy.

"He's been inside by himself ever since he heard," a man told me. "He is all tore up. He's been crying non-stop for over an hour." The man went inside the bus to tell Miloy we were there. After a few minutes, Miloy came out to us. Distraught, he still wanted to share his feelings.

"I just keep thinking about his little girl," Miloy said in a trembling voice with tears welled up in his red eyes. "I've always looked up to that man as a good family man and that's what America is all about."

Miloy stared off towards the speedway.

"We lost a great one today. The true cowboy of NASCAR is gone."

Another fan outside his RV told us how he was listening to Earnhardt's crew on the scanner.

"After that crash with Tony Stewart, somebody asked Dale about his car. Was it okay? He said, 'I'm not worried about that. Did everyone make it out of there?' "

We did multiple reports for the WSBT 11:00 News that night and I did a live shot with WISH-TV in Indianapolis about Earnhardt. When we finally got done, Rabold and I helped satellite truck operator Wilson Johnson tear down the cables and get his truck ready to travel back to South Bend. It was 2 AM by the time we were done. Before driving his truck away, Wilson walked back towards Turn Four and stood there and stared at the spot where Earnhardt had crashed.

We slept for just a short time and were back up early Monday morning to do day-after coverage. A local 7-11 operator in Daytona Beach told me that he had sold over 900 newspapers that morning. Many Earnhardt fans, desperate for the newspaper souvenir, went into residential neighborhoods and got papers out of driveways. Though they were ashamed of their actions, they had to read anything they could get about their hero.

The headline read: "Black Sunday".

We ran into Bob and Herta Johnson of South Bend, who have been to 13 straight Daytona 500s. Herta used to be a big Davey Allison fan. She even met him once. He died in a helicopter crash.

"I don't like to pick a favorite anymore," she told me. "I don't. That hurts too much."

We drove to the Speedway where Earnhardt fans brought flowers, caps and wrote notes by a fountain near the entrance. I interviewed fan after fan that wept softly as they tried to find the words to express their grief. One little four-year-old girl hugged her Mommy's leg as she cried near the flowers. Jeff Gordon and Rusty Wallace fans showed up to show their respect. An Earnhardt fan asked Speedway officials to get more poster board for fans to write on. "If ya'll ain't got any, I'll go across the street to K-Mart to get some for everybody," the fan said.

Personally, a lot of thoughts ran through my head as I did my job for the newscasts. I have been around death in racing. Years ago, I did stories on Billy Vukovich III. He died in a crash. In 1988 I interviewed Rich Vogler testing tires at Plymouth Speedway. He died the next year in a crash. One day they were here. Then they were gone. Good men. Hard men.

As I flew back to South Bend, I thought about Earnhardt and his son laughing before the race. A father's love for his son can be shown in many ways. Earnhardt the father showed his love by changing his hard-charging "win at all costs" style on the last lap to block other cars so that either his son or Michael Waltrip, who were running 1-2, would win. Waltrip had never won a Cup race. Many considered him a so-called "loser." Not Earnhardt. He hired him to drive one of his cars.

As South Bend came into view, the words of the woman who ran the motel we stayed in all week came back to me. As I was checking out earlier that day, she looked up at me and said, "You know, I just think God needed Dale to build a race track in Heaven."

When I got back to South Bend, we focused on newscast coverage for the early stages of the week. On Tuesday, our Question of the Day on our 5:30 Evening News was "Was Dale Earnhardt the Greatest Driver of All Time?" We got a large volume of calls. 68% said he was. 32% said he was not. We had many e-mails sent in throughout the half hour newscast:

I believe he was the best driver NASCAR ever had. You never knew what he would do in each race. It was fun to watch the way he raced. He was there for his fans to the end. He knew if it wasn't for the fans he wouldn't be where he was.—Cheryl

I think Dale was one of the best NASCAR drivers in its history. However, I believe A.J. Foyt is the best driver of all time. With numerous dirt track championships, a Daytona 500 win, and four Indy 500 wins.—Mark

I would imagine many Earnhardt fans will start following his son. Some might start rooting for Tony Stewart, since he has somewhat of a hard-charging style like Dale did. I'll bet a bunch start following Michael Waltrip because of the classy way he handled everything, and the nice things he said about Dale all week leading up to the 500. Michael Waltrip is a good guy.

It took me a long time to deal with all the emotions in me. Watching him crash and die was hard enough, but interviewing his loyal fans that night and the next day also took a tremendous toll. People that don't follow racing or scoff at it have no idea how much fans love and respect the drivers. In Earnhardt's case nobody else had fans like him. They loved the man, flaws and all. He was a racer. Period. I thought a fan said it best when he said, "If Dale could talk about the crash that killed him, he would say it 'was just one of them racing deals.'"

PAUL HARTLAGE

Many of us are fortunate to have a mentor in life, someone that takes us under his or her wing and teaches us and gives us opportunities. Paul Hartlage was my mentor in broadcasting. I was very, very fortunate to learn the business from him and to be his friend.

It was 1984, my final year of college. I had decided to go into TV News broadcasting as a sports anchor. For two years I had busted my tail at the University of Mississippi campus TV station. I was on the right path. I just needed an internship at a local TV News station, and then I would be ready to go get a job upon graduation.

Through the excellent Journalism Staff at the University of Mississippi, I was able to get a summer sports internship at one of the TV Stations in nearby Memphis. In the spring, I drove up to WHBQ-TV to be interviewed by the Sports Director, Paul Hartlage, and the news director, who probably had better things than sit in on intern interviews.

I drove to WHBQ and waited in the lobby for Paul. I didn't know much about him. He was new to the market. Being a college kid, I hadn't watched too much local news in the last couple of years. I used to watch all the time in high school. Every night I watched the sports at 10:20, then "Gunsmoke" with Sheriff Matthew Dillon and Festus Hagen after the news.

In the WHBQ lobby, I heard Paul's booming voice at the top of the steps as he finished saying something before bounding down to meet me. He was a robust man. Stout. Strong shoulders. Stood about 6' 3". He seemed to me to be in his 30s. He had blonde brown hair with a strong Dick Tracy-like jawline, which always translates well on TV. As he reached out his hand, I braced for the "iron" shake. You know, the one where the person really grips your hand. Be ready, or your knuckles will crack!

"Hello there, Mississippi!" he said good-naturedly. He slapped his big paw on my shoulder and guided me up the steps and into the newsroom. We hit it off right away. I had the feeling he could work with anyone, and that he actually appreciated me being there. Sometimes, interns can be annoying fleas, but right from the start Paul made it sound like I would be of value to the sports department.

We sat in with the news director for about five minutes. He was a nice guy, but I was probably priority number 107 on his list for the day, so we moseyed along shortly. Paul guided me around the newsroom, and introduced me to everyone. We popped back into the small sports office, and talked. Paul told me I would do a little of everything. He emphasized that it was important that I not just wait to be told to do something. I needed to show initiative right from the start. At no time was I to resemble a bump on a log just *being there*. Everything went great and I was to start my internship as soon as my spring semester was over at Ole Miss.

Paul interviewing former Cardinals manager Joe Torre.
Ironically, both would go on to face cancer.

Paul had come to Memphis with a solid background in broadcasting. While in the Army, he was the sports director of the American Forces Television Network in Seoul, South Korea. After leaving the Army he became a sports anchor in Duluth, Minnesota. Most sports fans like sportscasters to express their feelings. Paul wasn't shy about doing that. In 1980, he supported the US boycott of the Olympics in Moscow.

"How can a man possibly say sports and politics don't mix when they allow national flags and anthems to be played?" Paul said on air.

From Duluth, Paul was hired by WISN-TV in Milwaukee where he was the weekend sports anchor. It was a nice job, but he aspired to be the main sports anchor in a good-sized market. His resume tape of his work in Milwaukee was impressive. It had clips of a well produced, thorough sportscast. It had stories he had done on the Packers and Brewers. It also had a series he had researched and done on steroid abuse, which was a fairly new thing in the mid 1980s. No doubt, it helped him get the job as sports director in Memphis. Paul was a cerebral sports anchor—one that liked sports, but kept it in context. He appeared to me to be a man that went to the front section of the paper first, but knew sports inside and out.

One of my first jobs under Paul was to go with sports photographer Ricky Briggs to cover Memphis Chicks baseball games at Tim McCarver Stadium. The Chicks were a double A minor league affiliate. My job was to climb the long ladder first that went to the top of the press box and then grab Rick's $50,000 camera as he climbed up behind me. Visions of me dropping it kept me highly focused during the exchanging of the camera at the top of the ladder.

We would sit there for four or five innings taping baseball hilites. At some point I would climb down and bring us back some hot dogs. When we would get back to the station, I would tell Paul the possible highlights for the sportscast that night. He would tell me which ones to go edit with Ricky.

One day Paul learned that the Cincinnati Reds were naming Pete Rose as player-manager. Paul knew that Don Kessinger lived in Memphis and that Kessinger was the last player-coach in the majors (he was with the Chicago White

Sox). Paul sent me to Kessinger's home to get his perspective on Rose.

Things were going along pretty routinely for me as an intern. I checked the AP wires. I made phone calls for Paul. Then one day my big moment came! The Memphis Showboats were the USFL pro football team in town. Remember the USFL? Donald Trump owned the New Jersey Generals. They had Herschel Walker. Jim Kelly was quarterback for Houston. Well, Memphis had former Alabama QB Walter Lewis as their star on offense. Reggie White, who would go on to the NFL, was the man on defense. Like a good sports director should, Paul had good contacts with the Showboats brass. Everytime I was around him and them, I could tell they really liked him, and probably favored him over the other media guys. Sure enough, someone in the Showboats front office called Paul with a tip. Walter Lewis, the star quarterback, had a thumb injury and was probably going to be out for awhile.

It was late in the afternoon. News time was getting close. It was too late for Paul to go do the interview because he had to anchor the sportscasts in studio.

"Charlie!"

I jumped.

"You and Ricky, get going! Get to the Showboats! Walter Lewis is hurt. Interview Pepper Rodgers (the coach) and get your butts back here for the 5:00."

Out the door we went like wild dogs hunting rabbits. Ricky had stubby legs and was not a man built for speed, but he knew how to scurry. It's amazing how fast news people can go when they have to. We drove like Dale Earnhardt, Jr. over to the Showboats camp and found Pepper.

He didn't know me from Adam. I fired off some questions about Lewis. I could tell the coach was really down. Losing a quarterback does that to a coach. The interview was short and sweet, and back we went to WHBQ. This time we drove like Tony Stewart. It just moments before the 5:00 sports. We went bounding in hollering "We're back!" Paul stormed out of the office and bellowed, "Cut me sound! About thirty seconds! Peppers' first answer! Whatever it is. Go. Do it. Now. Call the director with times."

We ducked into an edit booth and Ricky furiously cut the piece together for Paul. I sprinted with the tape to the control room and got it to the tape roller just a minute or so before Paul went live on air. The story went smoothly and a big scoop belonged to WHBQ.

WGKX-KIX 106
10th Annual Holiday Gala
1993

Paul with his wife Elaine
at a Memphis radio station Christmas party

119

Paul was pleased with what we had done. He believed in me, and saw potential. He trusted me to go out on a big story. We would often go out to eat between the 6:00 and 10:00 newscasts. He told me how he had met his wife Elaine when he was in the Army in South Korea. He always raved about their two young boys, Sander and Andrew. Gosh, how he loved them all.

Former Notre Dame Basketball Coach Digger Phelps used to teach his players about "the game of life." Paul did the same for me. We talked for hours about all kinds of subjects. He always listened intently when I talked. He cared about what a twenty-year-old had to say. He would disagree with me in a second if he felt I was wrong. He instilled me with broadcasting confidence and gave me a foundation to build my professional career. He told me everything to expect in the business.

Eventually, Paul let me do a story that aired on the broadcast. In many good sized markets like Memphis, interns are there to fetch burgers and that's about it. Paul saw potential in me, and gave me all sorts of opportunities. My first on-air story was a game report on a Memphis Chicks game. It was short and sweet. My southern accent was right out of "Dukes of Hazzard." I remember describing one of the Chicks players as Bill-eeeeeee Best. Not Billy Best. Instead of saying "can't" I said "kane-t." I never pronounced the "g's on the end of words like "fixing" and "going." Paul patiently went over my diction with me and started weeding out my southernisms over time.

Anyone who saw my standardized test score from high school would know I've never been the sharpest tool in the shed. For example, in 1984 the Olympic Torch was relayed through Memphis. Paul had me do a feature on the local man who would run with the torch. I asked Paul for ideas on a reporter "stand up" I would do in the story. He said I should go to a place on the road he would be running and reference the course.

Being dense, I didn't grasp that concept.

Photographer Ricky and I drove a long way outside of Memphis to a country road. The whole point of driving out there was so I could reference his course. So what did I say in the stand up?

"So-and-so is really looking forward to carrying the torch because it is a once in a lifetime experience."

Ricky never said anything, but he must have been thinking, "This kid made me drive way out here and he doesn't even talk about the course!"

Like I said, I wasn't the brightest bulb.

One of the highlights of my summer came when the 1984 US Olympic baseball team came to Memphis to play an exhibition game. Paul sent me out to interview some of the players. He suggested I talk to the big red head on the team, a kid on Southern Cal's baseball team. I did. The player was very nice to me and had a big, broad smile and broader shoulders. Name was McGwire. Mark McGwire.

Another memorable moment for me was getting to interview author Willie Morris in the lobby at WHBQ. His friend Rocky Miskelly brought him by the station. Willie had just written *The Courting of Marcus Dupree,* a remarkable book on the intense recruiting of Philadelphia, Mississippi running back Marcus Dupree and on the history of race relations in his home county. To this day, I truly believe had Marcus had better guidance, he would have gone on to be the best running back ever.

Paul made sure that all kinds of sports were covered. Pro Kick Boxing was pretty big in Memphis. He encouraged me to get out and do stories on Anthony "Amp" Elmore, who was the champ at that time. I got a "kick" out of kick boxing. I loved it. It wasn't silly like pro wrestling. The kick boxers beat the stew out of each other. After covering it, with all its high leg kicks, I always looked at boxing as rather bland. Boxers just slug each other.

One time Paul gave me the job to make sure Memphis State head basketball coach Dana Kirk was lined up for a live shot during the 6:00 Sports. The Tigers had a home game that night at the Mid-South Coliseum. Paul called Kirk and got him to agree to do the live shot. My job was to get him over to the courtside camera and 6:20 so that he could do a "talk-back" with Paul, who was at the WHBQ studio.

I found out later that Kirk liked to wait until the very last second to come out to the camera. Supposedly, he got a kick out of making the TV crews sweat a little. Well, when it got to be 6:15 and I couldn't find him, I panicked. The live interview was just minutes away and he was nowhere to be seen. I ran around like crazy. Finally, I went back to the camera at 6:19 and was getting ready to call Paul and tell him I couldn't get Kirk there. Seconds before the live shot, Kirk strolled out from the locker room and went straight to the camera. He put on the earpiece and did the interview. I just sat down and patted my heart.

Paul and I hit if off so well, that after my internship ended in August I still kept coming back to do stories for Paul's sportscasts. I was in my final semester at the University of Mississippi. I would drive up on Saturdays to cover college football games for WHBQ. I would stay at the station until 3:00 in the morning cutting three packages for him to run the following week. The station paid me thirty five dollars a report. One night I wearily left the newsroom and walked to the parking lot to find my car. It was gone. Stolen. Duh. Black Camaros tended to catch the eyes of car thieves in Memphis. It turns out the bad guys took my car and went and mugged someone. A bystander caught the license plate and called Memphis Police. There for awhile the police reports were that Charlie Adams was involved in a mugging. All this time I was sitting in an edit booth just editing away. They ditched the car after the mugging and I got it back in a few days. I was so overjoyed to have to pay the car pound a fee to get my stolen car out!

To start the ignition, the bad guys had hot-wired it. They hacked up where the key goes in, so for a few days, I had to hot-wire my own car to get it started. That got me odd stares from little old ladies as they watched me from sidewalks.

Paul was very upset about the whole thing and saw to it that parking lot security was increased at the station. If Paul had actually caught the pond scum that stole the car....

I tried my best to get a full time job with WHBQ sports. Paul lobbied the news director hard, but they did not want to add a 21-year-old. They felt I needed more experience. Paul then showed me how to put together a resume tape. During his dinner hour, he took me into the WHBQ studio and had me practice anchoring. He got the studio crew to come down and help me tape an anchor segment to have on my resume tape.

He wrote recommendation letters. He showed me how to look for sportscaster openings.

I ended up getting the sports director job at WTOK-TV in Meridian, Mississippi because of Paul's guidance. My resume tape had three stories that had aired on Memphis TV. That got me the job. The news director in Meridian was so impressed that I had done a lot of stories for a Memphis station. It wouldn't have happened if Paul hadn't encouraged me, taught me, and given me on-air opportunities.

Paul was intense. One time, my buddy Steve Garner visited me from St. Louis. Steve went with us to watch our WHBQ Softball team play a charity exhibition game. Paul was the pitcher and leader of our team. When we got to the game sight, the umpire did not show up. My friend Steve offered to be the home plate ump. Steve knew sports inside and out. He figured it would be a leisurely charity game and he would call an occasional strike or ball.

The author, Charlie Adams (Yankees cap)
stands next to his broadcasting mentor and friend Paul Hartlage.
Naturally, Paul was wearing a beer shirt.

Wrong. Appreciative of what Steve was doing, but intense at the same time, Paul gave him a hard time over any ball-strike calls. Poor Steve. He would call a ball and Paul would verbally let him have it from the mound. I was playing first base. Steve would look at me like, "I just wanted to help out...." I would just shrug.

After leaving Memphis, I saw Paul every so often, but my broadcasting work always reflected his influence on me. Not long after I left WHBQ Sports, the bright, aggressive and potential-filled John Koski filled my active role in the sports Department. He and Paul became very close. Professionally, they worked very hard and well together, raising the bar for Memphis local sports coverage. They also became very, very good friends, which made what happened so hard for John to accept. Here are John's reflections on Paul:

> "I was in the Liberty Bowl at the 1996 University of Memphis Spring Football game when Paul approached me and told me he had cancer of the esophagus. I couldn't believe it. It was surreal. Paul was a very big, strong guy, and I could tell he was relying on his own inner strength to deal with the shock. He didn't soften the blow. He told me it was a death sentence.
>
> Back in 1984 I approached Paul about becoming an intern at WHBQ in the sports department. I was working for WHBQ radio at the time (in sports) as a college sophomore. Paul welcomed me into the TV sports department and we became great friends. He treated me as the "third" sports guy almost from the start, which startled everyone including me. But it was great.
>
> Paul taught me a lot about the ins and outs of putting together a good sportscast, but more than any-thing I think Paul influenced me by encouraging and demanding a positive work ethic. When we faced a problem, we found a way to get it done. We took risks and thought big. We produced specials with multiple live cameras from the PGA Tournament in Memphis and a charity horse show. We covered high school sports bet-ter than anyone in the market. And we had a blast.

Paul liked a beer, or two, or more if you know what I mean. One night, when Charlie Adams was visiting, we went down to a place called Newby's near the U of Memphis campus and had a few. Paul had his share. Man, he could down 'em. Anyway, this jerk in the bar started giving Paul a rough time by calling him Stan Saunders, who was WHBQ's weekend sports anchor. Paul, as I remember, told the loudmouth he should shut up. The guy responded by blowing in Paul's face — as if he were going to spit on him.

Paul jacked him. Across the jaw. I couldn't believe it. I thought there was going to be a real bar room brawl, but the tensions died down quickly.

One time Paul set me up to be the victim of a practical joke. He set it up with none other than a guy named Charlie Bailey — who at the time was the head football coach at Memphis State. At that time, Bailey — who could kill a beer even faster than Hartlage — had experimented with a QB as a two-minute drill QB. This player had a particularly good game the week before and the fans were saying he should start.

Paul told me to do a story on it, but I whined that Coach Bailey was going to rip my head off when I asked him the question. Bailey was a big gruff at times. Paul told me to grow up, shut up, and do my damn job.

So, the time comes and I have Coach Bailey one-on-one. I said, 'So, Coach, uhh, are you going to continue to use Tim Jones as your starting quarterback?'

Bailey was ready.

'Koski, let me ask you a question. Are you going to continue to be the #*!#@*!! damn roving reporter around here??!!'

I was stunned. Bailey started to laugh. Then he looked in the camera and said, 'Hartlage, I got him!'

Paul was always very supportive of me. But I earned that support. I worked my butt off. I will always appreciate the opportunity he gave me to get on the air.

When our station was sold in 1990, they fired Paul. I always thought it was a goofy thing to do. The guy was the radio play-by-play man for the University of Memphis Tigers. He was well known and he cared. For some dumb reason they didn't see the value which to this day I think was crazy. They sent me out of the building to cover some mundane news story when they let Paul go. I think they were afraid I would get upset or something. I don't know. When I got back, they told me they were making me weekend sports anchor and promoting Stan Saunders to Paul's job. It put me in a tough spot. But Paul was very gracious in losing his job. He was classy that way.

When I left sports and got into management he remained supportive, and predicted I was on the fast track for general manager. I said he was crazy.

He hired me on to do the scoreboard show for the Tigers radio network, so we worked together again and I loved it. It was a blast. He was always calling me 'Jack Koski' on the air. In 1996, Paul was very sick when the college football season started. At the Louisville game Paul was being fed intravenously. He still called the game from an open-air booth in cold weather. When he got so sick that he had to miss several games he asked me to fill in for him doing the play-by-play. I was honored. I knew then why he loved the job so much. It is, perhaps, the best job in all of broadcasting. I felt guilty because I enjoyed it so much. I did five football games while he underwent treatment. By November, Paul was strong enough to call the Tennessee game.

The Tennessee game. A movie scriptwriter couldn't have come up with a better story. In front of a national CBS audience, the Tigers came from behind and stunned Peyton Manning and the mighty Big Orange on a last minute touchdown. The score was 21-17.

'Tigers win! Tigers win! The Tigers beat Tennessee!' Paul was so happy. I will always remember how thrilling it was to be part of that broadcast. Paul cut a deal to have me do live sideline radio reports, so it was just a perfect day. Unforgettable. Paul said, 'I'm just glad I was alive to see this happen.'

It was the first and only time the Tigers had ever beaten UT.

As college basketball season rolled around, Paul worked most of the games, but he was really sick. I still can't believe he worked through all of that. I filled in only one time during the 30-game season. By the time the conference tournament was played in St. Louis, this mountain of a man was reduced to a fraction of himself.

That April, we had a birthday party for Paul at his house east of Memphis. We talked about next season. He was planning to be ready for another football season. Then I got a phone call that he was back in the hospital about a week later. I went to see him, but he had lost his hearing. When he saw me, he said he couldn't talk right then. He died a couple of days later.

I never understood why Paul refused a funeral, or even a memorial service. To this day I would argue with him about that if I could — as weird as that sounds. If even for his Mom or Dad, so they would know how loved the guy was, or something to help with the pain of losing him. He said no way. His wishes were respected. Not even a memorial service.

This past February, I was promoted to general manager at WHBQ TV. The most poignant congratulatory note was from a man named Bob Lewis, who had been program director here for many years. The note simply said: 'Paul would have been proud.'

Paul was one of my best friends of all time. I think about him a lot."

Dave Woloshin has covered Memphis Sports for years. He hosts a popular talk show on WMC radio weekday afternoons and is the Voice of the University of Memphis Football and Basketball teams. He became close buddies with Paul back during the days Memphis had the USFL Showboats. He was one of Paul's closest friends. Dave has these memories of the one and only Paul Hartlage:

"The first time I ever got to know Paul was on a Showboats road trip to Washington, D.C. We had dinner with a new *Commercial Appeal* writer named Ron Higgins. We ordered beer to precede the meal. When it arrived, it came in a container that appeared to be a pitcher. It actually was an individual mug, but no one knew that at the time. Paul would always order two beers to start. Two mugs were placed by him. He picked up the first mug, and began to drink. That opened up everyone's eyes, thinking he was sipping from a pitcher that was to be shared by all. Higgins must have thought, 'O.K., I'll just grab the other one.' As he reached out, Paul grabbed his hand and said, 'Get your own.' The table went silent until all the other goblets arrived.

There was no one, not a single human being I've ever come across, who could imbibe beer like Paul.

Paul with the University of Memphis broadcast team and former Head Coach Larry Finch.

He also had to rank right up there in courage. During his final days he refused to give up doing the University of Memphis basketball games. One road trip to Nashville had us playing Vanderbilt in old Memorial Gymnasium. His broadcasting partner Hank McDowell picked him up at his house and drove him to Nashville. Paul lay down on the backseat for the trip. At Vanderbilt, there is a press row on the floor, but almost everyone except national TV has to go upstairs to the crow's nest of a press box. By the way, there is no elevator. Now, here's a guy who has gone from 289 pounds to about 120. The cancer he has is eating away at his esophagus, as well as his throat and stomach. The walk up the stairs took 45 minutes. It almost killed him. Somehow he found the energy to do the game. The walk down the stairs, through endless concourses, set him up to sleep all the way back to Memphis. But he refused to stop doing the games. Sometimes, during a game when they would take a commercial break, Paul would lower his head to the press table, close his eyes, and re-group. Then, when they sent it back to the game, he would spring back up to life, never missing a beat, and do the broadcast. It was truly amazing. The games kept him alive.

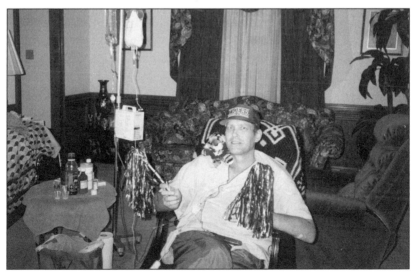

Despite aggressive cancer, Paul was determined to fulfill his duties as voice of the University of Memphis football and basketball teams.

The season ended in April. He died in May. I honestly believe if the season had lasted another year, he would have been around another 12 months.

Paul could be so deceiving. You wouldn't guess from his attitude outside work, by his approach to social events or his dress, that this was an organized, prepared guy. He was serious about his job. And he knew what was important, and what wasn't in every journalistic sense. He also knew one very important lesson that young sportscasters take a while to learn. Don't sweat the small stuff. The control room director of the newscast is going to screw up, hit the wrong button, and make you look bad on-air. The graphics guy isn't always 100%. The news director, usually a weird person anyway, invariably will take time away as weather went too long or decided not to give you that camera and photog you were promised for the Pulitzer prize interview you set up five months ago. Paul knew to care only about the things that he could control. He took that lesson, and applied it in his fight for life.

You won't find many like our friend Paul."

Paul faced death with courage and hope. He kept a saying on the wall that read, "In the face of uncertainty, there is nothing wrong with hope." Everyone was amazed at how he continued to keep living a full life in his final year. Columnist Geoff Calkins wrote, "He reminded us of an old truth: Dying is easy. Everybody does that. It's living that's the trick."

The treatments Paul got during his final year were incredibly hard, yet he kept going on. He was just starting a combination of chemo and radiation when he broadcast Memphis' big football win over Missouri. He vomited during commercial breaks, but never let the listeners know. After the game, the team gave him the game ball. The locker room was very emotional. Memphis assistant athletic director Bob Winn told *The Commercial Appeal* that after the game he followed Paul under the darkness of the stadium. He watched as Paul retched and cried, and then put his arms around him. It was all he could do.

In his final days of a courageous battle against cancer, Paul emcees the annual University of Memphis basketball banquet at The Peabody Hotel.

After he gutted his way through his final college basketball season as team announcer, the gravely ill Paul still fulfilled his role as emcee of the annual Tiger Basketball Banquet. He arrived at The Peabody by wheel chair, but stood to do his job that evening. He tried to keep his composure when reflecting on his ten years as Voice of the Tigers. He fought back tears when talking about his battle against cancer. The banquet crowd of over 350 gave him a thunderous standing ovation and the prestigious Dennis Dugan Memorial No. 1 Tiger Fan Award. The Tigers' Head Coach, Larry Finch, had just finished his final season at Memphis. He was being shown the door after a lot of years as player during their glory years, Assistant Coach and then Head Coach of the Tigers. Finch was obviously upset about his exit, but Paul's battle helped him deal with the hard feelings he had about those that had forced him out as coach. "I admire Paul so much for the fight he's putting up," Finch told *The Commercial Appeal.* "It really put the things in my life into perspective. I'm talking about a job, and here he is fighting for his life. I love that man."

Paul was 43 years old when he died. His wife Elaine Hartlage is now a flight attendant for United Airlines. She flies all over the world for them. Their boys are doing just great! Paul and Elaine instilled a tremendous sense of respect for others in their two children. They supported them and smothered them with love. Andrew is at Harvard. Pre-Med is his focus.

He wants to do research on cancer.

Sander is going into his freshman year at the University of Tennessee. He will study engineering.

Paul is buried in the military Veterans cemetery in his hometown of Minneapolis.

Ever the loving father, Paul with his boys
Andrew and Sander (now grown).

THE ELMWOOD REGULARS AND BAD, BAD SAND

"Where friends come together...to lose to Wil Hampton in golf!"

Every August, my longtime friend Wil Hampton (sports director at WISH-TV 8 in Indianapolis) has what he calls The Elmwood in central Indiana. I guess you would call it a golf tournament, except that half of the people in it only play golf a few times a year, so there's not a lot of real golf being played. There's no real chance of it being added to The Masters, US Open, PGA, and British Open as a Major tourney. Wil has The Elmwood as a way to bring longtime friends together every year. He also likes to win at golf, which is why, I think, the field is filled with pitiful to mediocre golfers. He selects the field. No one else is involved in the selection process.

For a long time he would invite a slew of his relatives from St. Louis. They were great folks to be around, but had no business swinging a golf club. They really came for two reasons: to see relatives, and for the Saturday night bonfire. On the golf course, they were a hoot. One time a fella drove a golf cart slap into a creek and turned it over. Exasperated, Bill finally organized a separate tournament for them earlier in the summer. He calls it The Quirk Cup. Linda Quirk, who set the Elmwood record for worst round with a 176, is much more comfortable in that event.

For years, I have asked if I could bring a friend to play in The Elmwood. I might as well ask if I could fly the next space shuttle. Wil always asks me what kind of golfer my potential guest is. I always say, "Oh, he shoots in the 90s. He's a good guy, though, and would be a lot of fun at The Elmwood, Wil."

Not a chance. Wil sees someone who shoots in the 90's as someone who could get hot for a couple of days and give him a run for the championship. Now, if I suggested bringing a friend that was on a life support system to play, Wil would probably agree, as long as that person brought some beer. All I know is that in almost twenty years I have never been able to get anyone I know into The Elmwood. Wil shoots in the high 70s and low 80s. For him to win every year, he's got to make sure the field is filled with hackers and golfers that will self-destruct at some point (like me). That always works, except for the years his brother-in-law shows up. Joe Weaver is his name. A consistent golf round is his game. Wil has to let Joe play because Joe is Wil's wife Becky's brother and Wil wants to have regular "relations" with Becky. Joe lives in Mississippi, so he only plays The Elmwood every few years. When he does, he becomes a Par Machine, nips Wil for the championship and drives back down to Mississippi with the first place plaque. That sends Wil into a year of misery until the next year's Joe Weaver-less tournament when Wil can beat the stiffs and regain the crown and the glory that he feels goes with it.

The Elmwood is a two-day golf tournament. For years we played in Muncie. Muncie is where the fella drove the cart in the creek and turned it over. I think the golf course managers are glad we've not played there much since. Wil is a cracker-jack sportscaster. When he became the main sports anchor at WISH-TV 8 in Indianapolis, we started having The Elmwood all over the place in central Indiana. Moving the Elmwood location around helps Wil. He's able to play the courses like crazy all summer, and then bring us all in August and compete with us on a course we know nothing about.

Wil starts his mind games months ahead of the Elmwood.

"Charlie, I think this is your year. You've got the swing. This is your year. You just need to keep hitting it long off the tee. I don't have that power game you do...."

Wil knows darn well that my long drives don't necessarily land on the fairway they were intended to. He knows in The Elmwood penalty strokes count, and ol' Charlie's weakness is out of bounds. He's notorious for having The Elmwood on courses with adjacent houses.

One year, on a house-surrounded course, I was leading the tournament. No, we weren't getting ready to tee off the second hole! We got to this par five and Wil softly mentioned how a long drive really helps on a par five. I went into my "Grip it and Rip it" mode and promptly hooked one onto somebody's chimney. Poof! There went my Elmwood chances. Again! I was steaming. Nobody said anything in our group, but there were carpenters about 100 yards behind us working on a roof. They were making some noise, so I turned around and started yelling at them!! "ALL YOUR NOISE MESSED UP MY SWIINNNGG!!!!"

Actually, my selection of words was a little different than listed above. Of course, their noise had nothing to do with my error-filled swing. I just needed to vent. They stopped hammering and just stood there for about ten seconds looking at me. They probably figured I was working on my seventh "cold one" so they got right back to hammering. Wil then stepped up and hit one of his annoying, robotic 210-yard drives right down the middle.

Sand traps are also my demise at The Elmwood. I have a mental problem when it comes to sand traps. Maybe its because I have never learned to hit out of them or have never practiced hitting out of them. Whatever, I always end up in a few in The Elmwood. One time, on some course near Noblesville, Indiana, I plunked one right in the sand. It had been raining a few days before The Elmwood, so the sand was soggy. I got in there, scrunched my shoes in the sand, bobbed and wiggled, and promptly skulled one out onto the side of a golf cart 50 yards away.

My temper erupted again and I came out of there spitting fire. "THAT TRAP HAS BAD, BAD SAND IN IT. THAT DOESN'T COUNT. THAT CRAP ISN'T SAND. IT'S MUD. THEY SHOULD COVER SAND TRAPS ON DAYS AFTER RAIN!!!"

"Gotta play by the rules," Wil said without making eye contact, while everyone else stared at the grass.

Have you ever had a time in your life where you wanted to murder someone? That right there was my time.

I sent my sand wedge on a 20-yard flying journey. It bounced off my cart and almost went back in the bag. The course golf pro, who happened to let us play free, was within earshot.

For a number of years I finished fourth in The Elmwood. That was my lot in Elmwood life. Unfortunately, in 1999 I was so bad that I got the dreaded "Should Have Gone Fishin' Award." It's a long trophy with a rod and reel pasted to it. Some truly awful golfers have won it in the past. Wil's brother Rob, who swings a golf club like a man trying to beat ticks to death, has won it a lot. His friend Bill Ault, who is a great business-man, but will only break 100 in his life if he quits after nine holes, has won it. Last year, I deserved that award. I hit drives onto rooftops, three-putted, skulled chip shots, and sailed nine-irons over the greens into the woods. I got to keep the cumbersome plaque for a year.

Elmwood dictator Wil Hampton (blond hair, glasses and beer gut) and some of the Elmwood Regulars.

Hampton devotes a room of their house to his Elmwood memorabilia. I can see Jack Nicklaus doing such a thing, but Hampton??!! From his Elmwood office inside his sprawling estate in Noblesville, Hampton recently penned these reflections for this book:

"The Elmwood started in 1980 in Muncie. Kerry Drayer, now of Fort Wayne, won the first one. Drayer hit a 15-foot side-hill curler to win by one stroke on #18 at Elks Country Club. Actually, his win assured us of having another tournament the next year, because I had to win. Kerry and I still wonder if I had won the first one, would we have had a second?

We played the 1987 Elmwood on my wedding day in Tupelo, Mississippi. We got up so early that we had to wait for the sun to come up while standing on the first tee. Joe Weaver won on the day he became my brother-in-law. I remember when Becky walked up the aisle and I greeted her at the altar. I whispered to her, 'Joe won.'

At that moment my bride realized how important the Elmwood was.

The dastardly Weaver won again in 1988 and 1997. He's the only player in tournament history to win every Elmwood he has entered. I have won 16. I repeat. I, Wil Hampton, have won 16. Kerry Drayer has one, and Frank Cross has a still-disputed championship. Did I mention that I have won 16 Elmwoods? 16. Sixteen.

The greatest tournament was in 1988. Joe Weaver and I were tied after the opening round. We were still tied after 33 holes of the 36-hole event. I choked on hole 16 at Cardinal Hills in Muncie with a double bogie seven. I still blame it on my brother Rob for rattling up in a golf cart as I was hitting my third shot. He wanted to see who was winning.

I guess he found out. Weaver ended up winning by two strokes.

The greatest shot in Elmwood history was my brother Rob at the ninth hole at Crestview in Muncie. While lying on his stomach, he knocked a ball out from under a bush. It rolled out of the rough, over a hill, on the green, and in the hole from about 60 feet!

The Elmwood Invitational got its name from the name of the barn where my parents lived (Mom's still there). The first trophy was stolen from a Burris High School Trophy Case.

My father, John Hampton, played in several events, but in 1995 started hitting a ceremonial "first ball." He always seemed to hit it right down the middle and it was a great way to start the tournament. After Dad passed away in 1997 I thought about having Mom, or maybe my son John (named after Dad) to hit the first ball. But I wanted to keep Dad involved. So, for the past two years, and for every year from now on, a player is allowed to ask Dad for help. On the first tee of the first day, each player, after hitting a flub shot (there are a lot of those) can ask, 'Mr. Hampton, may I please play another?' Then the player can hit a mulligan.

I still miss my Dad very much and that first is very emotional for me. I had tears in my eyes in 1998 and also struggled with emotions last year. But both years I played my first shot. Thanks, Dad.

The Elmwood is where good friends get together once a year to share old stories and play some decent golf. We've made it through marriages, the birth of kids, job changes, evil class basketball in Indiana, and toughest of all, Dad's passing. It's getting tougher and tougher every year to keep it going. This will be our 21st annual...Charlie's year to win!"

Yeah, right. The 2000 Elmwood was in August. One of the traditions is biscuits and gravy before the first round. It was a fine tradition when Mr. Hampton made the gravy. Sadly, Wil has started making the gravy to continue the tradition. Wil's gravy looks like the remains of a carp that has been run over by a school bus. I went heavy on the biscuits and laid off the gravy. I think Wil made the gravy so that his competitors would be pooting all through the first round.

Wil lined us up to play at Prairie View in Noblesville. He had played the course all summer. We hadn't seen it until we drove to it. Hampton hurried us on and off the driving range so that we couldn't get our rhythm. He did take time to talk with the lovely wife of Colts Tight End Ken Dilger on the driving range. Heidi said, "Oh, how nice," when Wil kept telling her that he had won The Elmwood 15 times.

On the first tee, Wil announced that I was the only golfer that had invoked the tradition of *"Mr. Hampton, may I please hit another?"* EVERY year since that tradition had started. I winced. Embarrassed by my yearly first tee woes, I hit a half-decent drive down the middle and didn't have to look to Heaven to ask for another drive. I certainly was thinking about Mr. Hampton, though.

Wil went out and established a substantial lead of 13 strokes. It was a brutally humid day. Kerry Drayer, who was turning 40 that week, wilted and almost melted. Kerry goes to bed about 8:30 every night. He's the only guy that has a remote chance at beating Hampton most years, but Kerry is aging and withering He's more concerned about going to bed early and getting fiber in his diet than beating Hampton.

My most significant accomplishment of the first day of Elmwood 2000 was stepping on a sand rake and twisting my ankle. I almost fell into the trap. I did win the Long Drive hole. That was an amazing accomplishment for me. I can hit it long, but I rarely keep it in the same fairway, or same county.

The second and final round was at Bear Slide in Cicero, Indiana. Again, Wil gave us minimal driving range time. With a whopping 13-stroke lead, Wil teed off first and sliced one into the water.

"Who was moving behind me?" he barked. Wil then started carrying on about the peripheral vision he developed as a basketball player as a kid and that he could see all around him. Like we really cared about his gift of peripheral vision. He bellyached about the movement causing him to slice. So, we got to the green and Wil missed a six-foot putt and ended up with a seven.

"I'm taking a six because somebody moved," he declared. He clearly made a seven with penalty strokes, etc. It's his tournament, though. All we could do was shrug.

On the second hole, I hit my drive up into that fescue weed/grass stuff. Riding with Muncie lawyer Joe Hunter, I got an iron and putter out and told him to go on. I would meet him at the green. I didn't find my ball in that stuff, but located a higher quality ball and declared it my ball. I wacked the ball out of the jungle stuff and marched to the green. Unfortunately, I left my putter back in that stuff and lost it. So, for the rest of the round I putted with a one iron or three wood. Wil said I couldn't borrow a putter at the turn because "Everyone would be disqualified because of rules." I looked like an idiot putting with a three wood.

At the end of 18 holes, I was tied with my cart partner Joe, an avid Colorado Buffaloes football fan. Wil declared that Joe and I would have a one-hole playoff for third place. We marched to the first hole like some junior imitation of a playoff at The Masters. Wil and Kerry were our gallery. They established Joe as the favorite because "of my lack of mental toughness." Much to my surprise, I hit my one iron straight as an arrow down the fairway. My wedge went to the green and I two-putted for par. Joe, stunned by me actually hitting good shots, made a double bogey. Forevermore he will be branded as "The man who lost to Charlie in a playoff." That is such a shameful label that he will probably move to North Dakota and practice law there.

After every Elmwood, Bill has an awards ceremony at our traditional bonfire. In 2000, he gave Joe Hunter the "I Should Have Gone Fishin' Award" for losing to me in a playoff. Wil then verbally scolded me for having not engraved my name in the traveling trophy. I had won it in 1999 for being absolutely dreadful. I never did go by a trophy shop and get them to add my name to the dubious plaque. I also accidentally knocked off the fishing lure that was next to the fishing pole on the plaque.

I told Wil that a year is just not enough time to get my name engraved on the plaque AND to glue another lure on it. Irritated with me, Wil had threatened to give me the award again this year. Instead, Joe got it and carted it off to his car trunk.

As we were all leaving I asked Joe to have my name engraved for the '99 award and to please buy another lure.

"I'll pay you a few bucks next year, Joe."

About the Author

Formerly the sports director for WSBT-TV in South Bend, Indiana, Charlie Adams is now the Saturday and Sunday morning news anchor for the CBS affiliate. In addition to his work in the South Bend market, he has worked in the broadcasting field for 17 years, with stations in Memphis, Tennessee; Bakersfield, California; New Orleans, Louisiana; and Meridian, Mississippi. He has won the Golden Microphone award three times, as well as an Associated Press/Broadcast Division Sportscaster of the Year award.

Born on July 9, 1962 in Oxford, Mississippi, Adams went on to graduate from the University of Mississippi with a degree in Elementary Education. He now has two children, Jack and Abigail, and resides in South Bend.

A popular and experienced guest speaker in the Michiana area, Adams is currently arranging a series of motivational seminars through Jill's Rubber Chicken Circuit. If you would like more information on inviting him to be a guest speaker at your event, please contact Jill Langford at (219) 299-9278.

I Didn't Know You Were So Tall! is his second book, following 1998's *Travels with Charlie*, also published by Diamond Communications.